WOMEN
WHO RUN WITH THE
POODLES

"Thank God women have come to their senses and stopped running with wolves and have taken up with poodles. A witty, delightful book."

Wendy Wasserstein

"Barbara Graham is the Fran Lebowitz of the New Age."

Dan Wakefield

"Graham has written a brilliant, side achingly funny satire of our times and ourselves. Grab this book and run with it."

Barbara Lazear Ascher

"Pack this book for the 'Hilarity Therapy' intensive at your next Solstice Gathering for Women Who Take Themselves Too Seriously."

Kate Clinton

WOMEN
WHO RUN WITH THE
POODLES

*Myths and Tips for Honoring
Your Mood Swings*

BARBARA GRAHAM
ILLUSTRATED BY VICTORIA ROBERTS

AVON BOOKS ◆ NEW YORK

For
Hugh Delehanty, the one,
and
Amy Hertz, one magnanimous babe

WOMEN WHO RUN WITH THE POODLES is an original publication of Avon Books. This work has never before appeared in book form.

AVON BOOKS
A division of
The Hearst Corporation
1350 Avenue of the Americas
New York, New York 10019

Text copyright © 1994 by Barbara Graham
Illustrations copyright © 1994 by Victoria Roberts
Cover art by Victoria Roberts
Inside cover author photo by Clay McLachlan
Published by arrangement with the author
Library of Congress Catalog Card Number: 93–42270
ISBN: 0–380–77632–4

Library of Congress Cataloging in Publication Data:

Graham, Barbara, 1947–
    Women who run with the poodles / Barbara Graham : illustrations by Victoria Roberts.
        p.   cm.
    1. Archetype (Psychology)—Humor.   2. Women—Psychology—Humor.
3. Wild women—Humor.   I. Title.
PS3557.R184W6 1994   93–42270
818′ .5407—dc20   CIP

First Avon Books Trade Printing: June 1994

AVON TRADEMARK REG. U.S. PAT. OFF. AND IN OTHER COUNTRIES, MARCA REGISTRADA, HECHO EN U.S.A.

Printed in the U.S.A.

ARC 10 9 8 7 6 5 4 3 2 1

Acknowledgments

To Mark Matousek—titlemeister and soulbrother who believes in me and keeps me honest—deepest love and thanks.

Bouquets of love and gratitude to my heroic agent, Sloan Harris, the best blind date I ever had.

More bouquets to everyone else who threw in their two cents: Rachel Lehmann-Haupt, Sheldon Lewis, Marcia Lippman, Belinda Luscombe, Ellie McGrath, Richard Rosen, Dan Wakefield, Steven Winn and especially my editor, David Highfill, a real prince who got it all, right from the start.

Supreme thanks to Victoria Roberts for being a genius.

For undying support and ancillary services rendered during the writing of this book, big, sloppy poodlekisses to: Abdi Assadi, Andrea Balis, Annette Breindel, Anna Christensen, Paula Cizmar, John J. Delehanty, Mark Epstein, Florence Falk, Audrey Ferber, Joan Goldberg, Frank Lipman, Louis Morhaim, Peggy Northrop, Laura Nurse, Marlene Provizer, Janice Rous, Sylvia Rubin, Rosemary Sussillo, Peter Tadd and Betty Wood.

Many thanks to the folks at the Millay Colony for the Arts for setting me loose on Edna's farm.

To Michael Rubin, who believed in me before I did, I am eternally grateful. I only wish he were here so I could toast him with an obscenely expensive bottle of champagne.

Love to Irene and Bernie and all the rest of the Glicks, Grahams and Kopelmans from whom I inherited my smartmouth—especially my brother, Richard, a master trickster in his own right.

As for my son Clay, a certified wonder, thanks for everything.

Contents

Part Three
Poodlewoman Meets Iron John

Epilogue

The breed is no nincompoop, being extraordinarily intelligent and standing no nonsense from anyone.

HUBBARD, *The Observer's Book of Dogs*

La Poodela

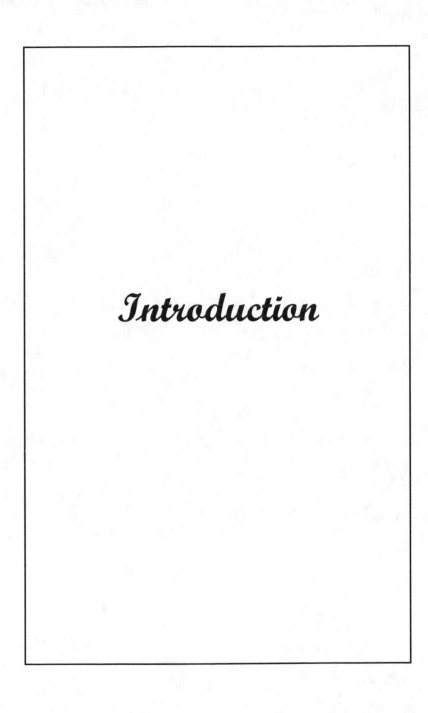

Introduction

An Open Letter to My Womansisters

Believe it or not, I used to be a self-help victim. A hapless seeker trapped on the treadmill of self-improvement. For years, I left no stone unturned. I perfected my orgasm. I fell in love with myself. I got in touch with my shadow, my inner child, my past lives, my power animals, my Higher Self, my lower chakras and my former husbands (they owed me money and as soon as I got in touch with my rage, I went after them). I learned how to rebirth, rebreathe, meditate, communicate, have meaningful dreams and walk on hot coals.

I thought I was healed. Whole. I mean, never before in this lifetime had my inner selves been on speaking terms with each other *and* my mother. The day had come for me to burn my New Age catalogues. No more workshops. No more weekends wailing and flailing on foam mats in moldy

Love Yourself

basements conducting an archaeological dig of my soul. I was ready to party. And shop!

But just as I was about to hit the stores running, I heard the news: A hot new archetype—the Wild Woman (WW)—was on the loose and creating a stir in the female psyche.

I was distraught: *My* WW was nowhere to be found. Did this mean I still wasn't whole? Did it mean weekends in caves howling at the moon with my sister she-devils? Was I being called upon to buy drums instead of platform pumps? Don scruffy-looking skins instead of faux fur? Drink menstrual blood instead of margaritas?

Even though my Higher Self told my frightened inner child to chill, my inner adult took the high road and I took to my personal power center—my bed. I just couldn't cope with the crowds. I had too many inner selves and they were all starting to run together. Soon they'd have to attend a twelve-step program for codependent personality fragments. And now I was being asked to get in touch with my WW—mother of all inner selves!

It was just too much. In between banging my head against the glass ceiling at work, attending goddess ceremonies, recovering my self-esteem and healing the traumas and addictions that until around ten minutes ago I didn't even know I had, I didn't have a clue how I would manage. All I knew was I couldn't go on living if I passed up my one last hope for wholeness.

I lay in bed tossing and turning. It was a dark night of the soul that lasted for days. When finally I rose from my feverish slumber, the woman who stared back at me from the mirror was wild looking, disheveled, a half-mad creature dripping with secret womanwisdom. I knew at once it was she: my She-Wolf. My WW. My Inner Hag.

As I stood there hypnotized by her hoary presence, it slowly dawned on me: I *know* this chick. I've known her for as long as I can remember. Only the names I know her by aren't *La Loba,* wolf woman or wild woman. No, I know her by her other name. A name our well-meaning womansisters have tried to wipe out: bitch.

I couldn't contain my joy. I began to dance around the bedroom. She's back, I sang feverishly. The bitch-on-wheels is back! No more pretending we're rational or in control. No more mouthing the party line that PMS doesn't mess with our heads. Like, whoa! We're being called upon to drop everything and honor our womancycles. Our primitive, unpredictable, unruly selves. Forget the fast track, the mommy track, being thin and having it all. At last, we celebrate the untaming of the shrew!!!

"Take your hands off me!" I screamed at my husband. "Make your own dinner!" I snarled at the children. "Walk yourself and scoop your own damn poop," I barked at

Gladys, the poodle. Cackling, I burst into a frenzied freedom dance. "Screw being nice!" I chanted wildly into the night. "Screw trying to prove and improve myself! Screw everybody!" When I finished, sometime after midnight, I stepped outside to bathe my she-lungs in the crisp night air. Gladys came with me—of course, no one else had walked her—and being a bitch who honors animal passions, I ripped the rhinestone choker from her neck and let her release her steaming she-bowels on Mr. Tortelli's dichondra.

The moon was full. We started to walk, but—I'm not sure whether it was the magic of the moonlight or the mugger at our heels—before I knew it, we broke into a gallop that took us up and down avenues, across cul-de-sacs, through parking lots and in and out of malls. Suddenly a strange voice began shrieking through me: "Ethel schmethyl merman ho!" Panicked, I was powerless to stop it. Was this channeling? Had I been chosen as a vehicle for some Great Cosmic Message or was I on a one-way excursion to the nuthouse? I prayed for guidance. A word, a sign, anything. Just then, I raised my fearful eyes heavenward and saw a *woman* in the moon. She was wearing a spandex catsuit flashing with sequins. She smiled and waved as the strange voice issued forth from my she-throat once more: "Ethel schmethyl merman ho!" I knew in that instant that I was safe. Protected. Chosen. I looked up once more, just in time to see her wink at me before fading into the dark shadows of the moon.

Since then my life has never been the same. In one night I was transformed from a nice, well-meaning Patsy (not my real name) into La Poodela, the bitch who runs with the poodles. I returned home with Gladys just after dawn, our she-loins glistening with womansweat.

Now that I've been joyfully reunited with my WW—my Sacred Inner Bitch, as I affectionately call her—I can be silent no more. The time has come for me to share my womansecrets with my sisters—to let you know that you don't have to trade your satins and silks for smelly old pelts or your Fifis and Fidos for wolves. You too can open to Ethel. You too can become an empowered self-help survivor.

I pray that my tale inspires you and serves as a light to guide you in your sacred womanquest.

Ethel schmethyl merman ho!

La Poodela

Part One

I Am Poodlewoman, Hear Me Roar!

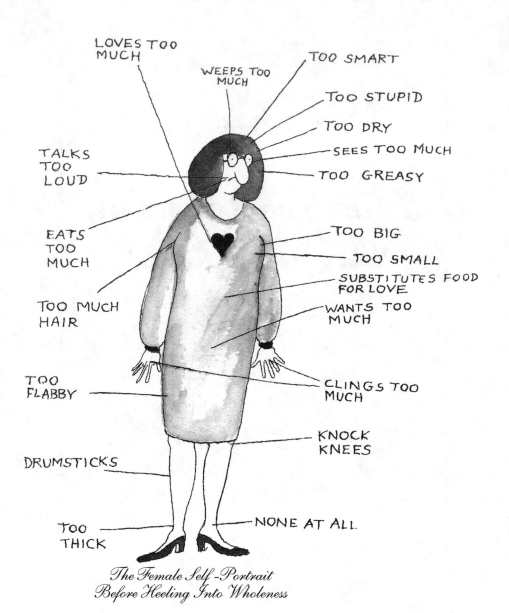

The Female Self-Portrait
Before Heeling Into Wholeness

Heeling into Wholeness

It's been a hair-raising millennium and, for those of you in touch with your past lives, a bad scene ever since the fall of Minos and the other Great Matriarchies, when she-women ruled the universe. Womansisters have been trying to take back the power ever since—but without much success. And that is for one reason and one reason only: *In our heart of hearts, we believe we're worthless, good-for-nothing she-devils.* Right after Minos, we got the idea that if we just lost ten pounds and stopped loving the wrong men too much (Genghis Khan, Woody Allen) or the right men too little (Mr. Rogers, Millard Fillmore), we'd be back on top. Numero Uno. But that, dear womansisters, is the whole horrible disgusting problem in a nutshell. We think we're supposed to be *better. More. Different.*

That's why Ethel, a former lounge singer who hails from Atlantis, has decided to break her fifty-thousand-year vow of silence and share her womanwisdom with us *right now* so we don't make the same stupid she-blunders in the next millennium.

ETHEL SPEAKS

"Lok hop arugula ho! Ancho cilantro jin shin ho! Ja-la-pe-ño! Ja-la-pe-ño! Ja-la-pe-ño-ho!" Translation: "Chill out, sister." (I *think*—though it's possible she's passing on a sacred recipe for chili con carne.)

THE INSIDE POOPER-SCOOP

So what gives? you're wondering. Is this just another one of those dogmatic programs like that wild wolfwoman deal? Why poodles? And what's a she-babe from Atlantis City got to do with *me?*

Well, I'm glad you asked. Because until that fateful night when I broke into a run with my poodle and spontaneously started channeling Ethel, I, too, was completely in the dark.

Imagine my surprise to learn that Ethel, the original La Poodela, was raised by poodles on Atlantis, when it was still part of Queens. Actually, Ethel was *adopted* by poodles after she ran away from the wolves her parents dumped her with in infancy—making her the first woman to run *from* the wolves.

"Dijon sourdough sinatra ho!" exclaims Ethel. (Translation: "Babycakes, I was born to live the lifestyle of the first leisure animal, not run with a pack of mangy pedadogues, n'est-ce pas?")

MEETING YOUR INNER POODLE

You may ask, why me? Why should I run with the poodles? Why not moo with the cows or bleat with the sheep? How will acting like a member of an alternative species change my life?

It won't. That's the point. Your life is fine the way it is—only you don't know it. How could you? Between the growth work and the grief work, you don't know whether you're coming or going or rebirthing. After all your past-life flashbacks, you're not even sure if you're living in America 2000 or Mesopotamia 90210. And now they're telling you to drop everything, head for the nearest cave and run with the wolves.

Well, I'm here to tell you it's okay to stay home.

I'll let you in on another little secret: evolution isn't such a terrible thing.

That's right.

All you have to do is look at a poodle: Poodles are descended from wolves. But they've *progressed.* They know the importance of a good haircut. They're sensitive to filth. And, they won't *tolerate* being ignored. (Much in the same way that all New Yorkers are Jewish, all poodles are female.)

It's not that they've lost the old hunting and retrieving instinct. No way. It's just that now they prefer to do their hunting and retrieving at Saks and Bloomingdale's instead of in the dirt.

Do you think any self-respecting poodle would give up its nice warm bed and fancy coat to run with the wolves?

Of course not.

Why should *you?*

PUTTING THE LID ON
SELF-IMPROVEMENT

The beauty of La Poodela's unique "Heeling Into Wholeness" program, as transmitted directly to me by Ethel (who was a good forty-eight thousand years ahead of her time), is that *you don't have to do anything.* No meetings, no fairy tales, no newsletters, no smelly pelts or embarrassing goddess ceremonies, no camping, no drumming, no screeching at the moon. (High heels, however, are a plus!) As Ethel says in her infinite womanwisdom: "The purpose of life is to *live* it."

I hear you saying, hey, La Poodela, why me? Why should I sign up for some stupid program that you can't even sign up for?

Well, I'm not going to twist your arm. Maybe *you* can live without "Heeling Into Wholeness." Maybe you're not ready to give up trying to be Ms. Perfect, Ms. Have-It-All, Ms. Attain-Enlightenment-And-Look-Like-Michelle-Pfeiffer-Too. Hey, it's up to you.

EIGHT WARNING SIGNS THAT YOU'RE A SELF-HELP ADDICT

But if you experience *any* of the following symptoms or tendencies, *this program is your only hope.*

1. You think shopping is a disease.

2. You've fallen madly, head-over-heels in love with yourself and think you make the cutest couple.

3. You think that if you just dropped a few pounds and did Kegels twenty times a day, you would have better, more mature *vaginal* orgasms like Freud said and then your sex life would be awesome and your husband would stop *schtupping* his she-rolfer.

4. You think love is a disease and death is just a phase.

5. Most of the time you feel like one of America's Most Wanted, a rotten she-criminal who deserves to be thrown in the pokey for being too fat, short, smart for your own good, stupid, tall, beautiful, ugly for words, emotional, thin (you wish), giving, bitchy, nice, needy, _____. (Fill in the blank)

6. When somebody screams at you and accuses you of being a self-centered, thoughtless she-turd, you agree and thank them for sharing.

7. You're positive that happiness is just a Sex-For-One, Ecstatic Shaman, or Hugging Your Inner Werewolf workshop away.

8. You think fairy tales hold the key to all your problems.

A WORD ABOUT FAIRY TALES

I would like to take this opportunity to speak out publicly against fairy tales and the fairy-tale mania that is endangering our nation's mental health. The next time you go to a shrink to talk about your *personal* problems and he or she launches into a long-winded discourse on Bluebeard or The Ugly Duckling, I strongly advise you to jump up out of your chair and take your Cinderella complex (the fear of being compared to a Disney character) elsewhere.

This is no joke. After just three sessions with a Jungian, Mrs. L. of Peoria, Illinois, drove straight to Orlando and viciously stabbed all seven dwarfs with a pastry knife for whistling "New York, New York" while vacuuming nonstop in her psyche. She's now on death row, praying for clemency from President Clinton—himself, the sorry victim of a "Ronald McDonald" weekend.

SETTING OUT ON THE PATH

Before embarking on your "Heeling Into Wholeness" journey, there are several important steps you *don't* need to take. For starters, there are no workshop wardrobe dilemmas (long flowered skirts vs gym clothes? Birkenstocks vs hiking boots? a G-string vs sweats for the sweat lodge?), no phone calls, no reservations, no deciding between dormitory-style accommodations or a private room, because there's *nowhere* to go. However, please note that the ritual wearing of high heels will be specified on a need-to-know basis.

HONORING YOUR MOOD SWINGS

A cornerstone of La Poodela's anti-self-improvement program is "Honoring Your Mood Swings." Sad to say, this ancient healing technique has garnered a lot of bad press ever since Delilah got her hands on a pair of scissors.

But let's face it: with a glorious spectrum of moods to choose from—anxiety, despair, jealousy, rage, disappoint-

Honor Your Mood Swings

ment, hysteria—what self-respecting woman wants to limit her options to plain old happiness? It would be like living in San Diego or wearing only puce. Where did we get the idea that we're supposed to be happy all the time anyway? (Don't think I don't have my government conspiracy theory: We'd need an expensive national retraining program for shrinks if people got hip to the fact that it's normal to be miserable at least 75% of the time.)

That's why the goal of "Heeling Into Wholeness" is to *learn not to be miserable about being miserable.* ("When you've got the world at your feet, why not just kick it?" queries Joan F. of Blanco, Texas.) In other words, don't worry, be miserable.

Next time you catch yourself feeling bad about feeling sad, remember the story of Cries Her Eyes Out, the Indian princess whose copious tears gave us rain, the seven seas and high-priced mineral water.

So kick back and relax. Que sera sera, babe.

SHRIEKING YOUR TRUTH

"Lordy! Lordy!" I hear you wail. "What do you mean, shriek my truth? How can I shriek my truth *when I don't even know what it is?*"

Good question, sister—but not all that good, because guess what? You just did it! That's the beauty part!

The point is, you can rest easy. If you honor your mood swings, your truth will follow. In fact, shrieking your truth will become so second nature, you won't give it a second thought. Which brings to mind one of our primo role models, the greatest she-babe of all time: Mother Nature. You think she plans *her* eruptions?

RECLAIMING YOUR SACRED
INNER BITCH

The *pièce de résistance* of my peerless program is "Reclaiming Your Sacred Inner Bitch." "Oh no, La Poodela," I hear you groan, "not another inner self!" And, hey, I dig where you're coming from. You've already got so many inner selves, you could start a bowling league. (Godforbid.) But, remember, this is La Poodela talking, okay? Let's show a little womantrust.

Anyhow, in my program, reclaiming your Sacred Inner Bitch is a snap, because the truth is, *she never left!* She's just been waiting in the wings! The only instruction is to unzip the Little Ms. Perfect costume you've been parading around in and let it fall to the floor, like a mink coat slipping off the shoulders of a stripper. (For the mythopoeically inclined, this primal exercise is called "Shedding The Faux Self, Vegas-Style.") The point is, toots, from now on your life is your own.

No more saying "yes" when you mean "no" or "c'mon down" when you mean "get stuffed." The time has come for you to reconnect your vital female organs—your mind and your mouth.

But what good is reclaiming your Sacred Inner Bitch without the support of your loved ones? There are many ways of breaking the news, but if you don't think you can get the message across without bursting into tears, apologizing or baking a pie, it's best to put it down on paper.

Here's an all-purpose sample letter, good for your husband, lover, boss, mother, agent, dry cleaner, personal trainer, doorman, hairdresser, gynecologist and other service professionals:

DEAR _____:
Surprise! It's not PMS, it's my womanature!

The Wholeness Hoax

Okay, so you're in touch with your Sacred Inner Bitch, you're getting good at honoring your mood swings and you're starting to really groove with envy, terror, despair and all the rest of the important, misunderstood emotions. What else is there? you ask. Am I whole yet?

The answer is no. You're partial. I'm partial. We're all partial. So why is everybody running around trying to get whole? Nobody knows for sure. Maybe because the planet is falling apart or there's nothing really good on TV.

If you ask me, it's all one giganto conspiracy by the weekend workshop people, who take their inspiration from the Calvinists. Only the idea here is, instead of getting your reward in heaven, if you howl and blubber on the weekend (and for one week in a bucolic setting where they serve mushy vegetarian cuisine concocted from no identifiable food groups in the summer), you'll heal all your pain and negativity, right here on the earth plane!

Are you with me?

The problem is, the minute you heal one part, your primal wound starts oozing someplace else, which they forget to mention in the brochures. Only by then you're hooked and you think, maybe just one more weekend, one more workshop, one more howl and *then* I'll be whole. But you're not, you're still partial—except now you're a helpless howling wholeness addict. It's gotten so bad, you need a special Tao-of-Weekends workshop just to help you decide what to sign up for.

The good news is that if you get off the merry-go-round and just say "no" to wholeness, you can end up like me: partial and proud.

Now don't get me wrong: You can howl all you want, just don't expect to get whole in this lifetime. Because the truth is, no matter how much you wail and flail and get in touch with the incredible inner you, you're not going to get completely whole because *the only people who are completely whole are also completely dead.*

Do you want to be like *them?*

The Unexpurgated Diary of a Helpless Wholeness Addict

So you're not convinced? You still yearn to be whole, but you're just not sure you can commit? To help you decide, here's a rare glimpse into an average day in the (current) lifetime of Aurora B., a helpless wholeness addict.

Morning

7:00 Wake up. Surprise and delight at finding myself in bed with *me!* Affirmation: "I am a magnificent womyn-being. Everything about me is potent and powerful, including my unique morning breath."

7:02 Brush teeth. Rinse with Scope.

7:04 Release my soul's golden elixir from deep within my sacred core. Decide *not* to flush in order to protect Great Mother's sacred core.

7:07 Journaling. Dreamwork. A forest. I'm in a little hut stirring a large pot of ewe stew when six burly men in burlap sacks burst through the door and stab me to death. Deep sobs as I release the pain of that unfulfilled lifetime. Whoa! I've already had my first major healing experience of the day and it's only 7:45 a.m.!

7:46 Urgent message from Narnar, my spirit guide, and zap! journaling turns into automatic writing.

8:19 Ecstasy! Spontaneous orgasm reverberates through my entire she-being (with a little help from my sacred automatic writing hand!). Oh, Narnar, you mischievous he-entity, you!

Past Life Flashback

8:27   As soon as my breathing returns to normal, I realize that a miracle has taken place. I've been chosen as a vehicle. Narnar wants me to go public ASAP, to share the sacred knowledge. Am instructed to do workshop and book: *Living on Neither Side of the Brain*. Have powerful vision, in which I *see* the title on the *New York Times* bestseller list. Oh, Diary, I'm finally ready to receive the prosperity of the universe! And the best part is, even though Narnar says I'll make millions, I'll be doing it for the good of all living beings, including paramecium! Make note to start calling agents later today.

8:56   All this planning to serve others is well and good, but *must* remember to take care of myself, too. Must replenish my deep well of givingness with simple beingness. Decide to take a little time out, just for *moi*.

8:57   Have incredibly therapeutic "Healing Your Innermost Inner Self" session with vibrator. Ooh-la-la!

9:48   Guess I got a little carried away. Rush to make my ten o'clock howl n' drumarobics class.

Afternoon

12:00   *Amazing* workout. Cleared a lot of old karma! My energy is so refined now, my vibrations at such a high level that I feel like I'm about to float away, so I treat myself to a double bacon cheeseburger to help ground me. It works!

1:30   Good thing I had an appointment for a high colonic right after lunch. Joanie, my excretotherapist (and a very old soul), compliments me on the "abundance" of my core.

3:16   Place calls to agents at ICM, CAA and William Morris. The sacred knowledge must reach the people ASAP!

3:37   Quel day! So much to do re: helping other beings—

but mustn't let myself put *them* first all the time! I must honor *my* biomoods too! Decide on a quick out-of-body jaunt to Bali for R and R, but something goes wrong because when I look down, I'm over Borneo instead. Below me three screaming anthropologists are being roasted on a spit over an open fire. It's a terrifying scene and, even though the natives can't actually *see* me, it feels like a *very* close call.

3:41 Back in my bed. Breathless. Shaking. Just what I need: another major trauma to heal! More grief work! What is the universe trying to tell me? That—bottom line—we're all somebody else's dinner? As soon as I have that incredible insight, I'm flooded with bright colors and flashing lights, so I know I'm on to something *big*.

4:00 Thank goddess I scheduled a check-up for today. Luckily, the appointment is with my Inner Internist, so I don't even have to leave my bed!

4:12 I'm blessed! Everything checks out perfectly, except my third eye, which is a tad nearsighted.

Night
5:11 I manage to squeeze in a little catnap before the phone rings. It's ICM. They're interested! And the best part is that it doesn't matter that I can't write. The guy says not to worry, nobody can anymore, but it doesn't stop them from getting their books published—in fact, *not* being able to write usually means you get a *lot* more money! I can't wait to tell Narnar.

5:23 Just as I'm about to open my channel and tune him in, the phone rings. It's Wanda. She goes on and on (and *on*) about her divorce, her sick mother, being laid off from her job, the foreclosure on her house, her cancer scare . . . Honestly! Some people are so self-absorbed. So codependent. It's not like I haven't had a rough day too!

6:13 I'm starving. Feel empty inside. But pristine. Like a clear mountain stream on the first day of spring. Send out for moo shu pork.

8:00 I can't believe how bad I'm being. I skip shamanic warrior ballet and just barely make it to my Gyno-American support group.

10:00 Marcie and I grab a quick wheat grass gimlet. She tells me about this incredible new therapy she's developed called Marciework. It combines Gestalt, reflexology, Sufism, finger painting, swimming with dolphins, cooing with doves, and humping with camels! Whoa! I'm sooooooo booked, but can't see how I can possibly let this one pass me by!

11:11 In bed, at last. Just the two of us. How I love these quiet, tender moments. Sigh. I hate to brag, but I do have the *cutest* inner child! I just love it when she falls asleep in my arms . . . Hey, I know what you're thinking, Diary. I *should* do my Tantric self-nurturing practice. But, after this morning, the batteries in my vibrator are shot and, frankly, I'm too beat to get out of bed to hunt for more. Anyhow, I've done enough healing for one day. Affirmation: "I am a whole and beautiful womynbeing." I just pray that if I work at it day and night, night and day, maybe someday (maybe even *this* lifetime!) I really will be whole . . .

The Unexpurgated Diary of a Partial Person

In case you're still on the fence about howling for wholeness or declaring yourself partial and proud, here's a peek at a day in the life of Lucille F., an uncontestably partial person.

Morning

7:00 Crack eyes open. Disappointed to discover that it's only just me and M. in bed, not A. Hepburn and G. Peck in *Roman Holiday*.

7:03 Affirmation: "I can get out of bed. I can stand up. I can make it to the bathroom unassisted."

7:05 To ponder at a later date: Why do all affirmations sound as though they were written by the author of *The Little Engine That Could?*

7:09 Eureka! Affirmation works! I pee without a hitch!

7:41 Mmmm . . . Love that first high colonic (double espresso) of the day!

7:43 Journaling—*Wall Street,* that is. Check stock closings to see if, by chance, I have any extra money to blow on crystal healing at Tiffany's.

7:44 Alas, the market dropped thirty points. About the only crystal healing I can afford is at Woolworth's.

7:48 High colonic works like gangbusters!

8:14 All of a sudden, getting dressed, powerful, mythopoeic images from last night's dream come flooding back. Images of swimming with Dolphins! We're in the ocean off Miami Beach—all *eleven* of them and me!—naked, frolicking in the surf when, all of a sudden, Dan Marino tackles me from behind. At first, I feel like I'm going to drown, but then I realize I can breathe underwater. We have unbearably hot sex. The entire team, plus an oceanful of real dolphins, crowd around and watch us, spellbound. I wonder what this means?

8:28 Incredibly horny, but M. has already left for work and L., my Higher Power, expects me to show up for a client meeting at 9:30, so I'm screwed. (I wish!) No time for even a *little* playful diddling of my favorite chakra.

9:16 Pass big shoe sale on my way to work. Run in and impulsively buy *two* pairs of leopard pumps. Whoa! It's just after nine, and already I've had my first major heeling experience of the day!

11:09 A spontaneous past-life regression when A., my former husband, calls to tell me he's in recovery from his sex addiction. Now, instead of schtupping every nymphette in the Western Hemisphere, he spends fourteen hours a day drinking coffee and *talking* about it. And, because he "still cares deeply" about

Near Death Experience

me, even though our marriage was "a toxic waste dump of pain and rage in which both our inner children really needed a mommy," he wants me to know that I'm always in his prayers. Oh, goody.

Afternoon

12:46 Have near-death experience (NDE) trying on bathing suits during lunch.

1:04 Admit that I am powerless over my addiction to eating. Take solemn vow (with saleslady as witness) to abstain from food for the rest of my life.

1:33 Uphold vow for twenty-nine minutes.

1:34 Wolf down hot dog from suspicious-looking sidewalk concern. Retake vow, with vendor as witness.

2:14 Intense biofeedback from hot dog: stomachache, belching, repeating on me.

3:38 Fantasize about going on retreat to my personal power center (bed) for a nice, midday out-of-body experience (nap).

3:39 No dice. My Higher Power bursts into my office, snickering. Suggests that the proposal I turned in yesterday was the result of automatic writing. Wants it redone ASAP.

3:41 Close door and treat my Sacred Inner Bitch to ninety seconds of automatic screaming.

Night
6:19 Late for enlightenment. Narcisso scolds me, but does the job anyway. I pay him $250 for hair that is now the exact color of Mandarin Orange Slice.

8:59 On the way home, I ask my Higher Self what message the universe is trying to send me. Her response: Enlightenment doesn't come easy. It can take several tries—and many years of sitting still—to get just the right shade of blond.

9:23 Homeopathy, at last! M. hands me a vodka gimlet and remarks that my hair looks "vibrant."

9:26 Look in mirror and do a little spontaneous grief work.

9:32 M., soulmate extraordinaire, whips up divine mushroom risotto. Break vow again.

10:45 M. grabs me from behind (just like Dan Marino!).

10:51 Incredible healing workout between the sheets of our personal power center. Mmmm . . . *Better* than *Roman Holiday.*

The Incredible Inner Yous

Then there's that other crazy can o' worms: the inner you. The big surprise here is that there *is* no inner you. There are inner *yous*. (That's why so many highly evolved people walk down the streets of our nation yelling, "Hey, yous!" They were hip to this stuff long before the whole weekend thing got started.) Anyhow, the deal here is that in order for you to become whole—or, let's just say, less partial—you have to reclaim all the sawed-off parts of your she-self. The hitch is, the second you say ho! to one part, another part pops right up—sort of like a constantly expanding universe, only instead of quarks and black holes, there's this cast of zillions multiplying inside your womanhead.

So why not just let sleeping inner selves lie? A right-on question. The problem, according to the grief-'n'-growth mafia, is that it's your unloved and abandoned inner selves that cause all your pain. And the only way to heal is to give them a name and hug them on the weekend in a large group of strangers at an airport Holiday Inn.

Got that?

So why bother, you ask? Why not just slip into a pair of high heels and head for Bermuda? Because if you ever stop to think about it—for even one second—you can't help wondering how a sister can get whole by breaking herself into a bazillion little sub-personality fragments, now can you?

The scary part is, nobody knows the answer to this question—not even Doktor Carl Jung, infamous he-father of the inner self.

DEAR DOKTOR JUNG:

You would not *believe* what goes on in your name. I suggest you consult your Inner Headhunter and pick a channel pronto before your archetype-happy followers turn us all into a bunch of whacked-out multiple personality cases.

SIGNED,
LA POODELA

This is no joke. In fact, several alarming cases of inner-self-induced psychosis, accompanied by low inner-self-esteem, have recently been reported in the literature.

Take my dear friend Bettye Sioux W. of Marin County, California. On a recent trip to Manhattan, she completely lost it over dinner at Le Cirque. Poor thing, she couldn't even order: her shadow demanded well-done dark meat, her wild woman howled for moose carpaccio, her crone pled for rice pudding and her wounded inner child threw such a tantrum that Bettye Sioux and her entire mewling mob were forcibly removed by Boris, the restaurant's burly *outer* bouncer.

Let this be a cautionary tale.

YOUR OWN PERSONAL PANTHEON

But, if after all this, you still can't resist saying ho! to the wacky crowd within, why not at least reclaim inner selves

The Inner-Self Hall of Fame

that meet *your* needs and compensate for *your* inadequacies—not mine, not your astrologer's, not even Doktor Jung's. (You might be wondering just exactly which self does the reclaiming—the whole you, or one of your sub-personality fragments, such as your Inner Hostess?—but this question is completely pointless and unanswerable, even by Ethel.)

The point is, who do *you* want at your inner dinner party? Here are some possibilities.

Inner Tina Turner. The Wild Woman herself. Turn up the volume and let yourself howl down. Your Inner Tina represents your fierce creativity, your fiery sexuality, and your earthy goddess womanpower. Reclaim her and you won't be singing backup for long.

Inner Sugar Daddy. Since wholeness depends on integrating the masculine with the feminine, why not pick some suave and well-heeled guy who'll not only protect you from the monsters who haunt your psyche, but will also set you up in a swanky pied-à-terre?

Inner Mother Teresa. Give yourself a break. With so many inner selves vying for your attention, it wouldn't hurt to have one who is self*less*, unconditionally loving and not repulsed by your thighs, your premenstrual acne or your stubby fingernails. Believe me, she's seen worse on the streets of Calcutta.

Inner Internist (board certified). How often do you wake up panic-stricken at 3 a.m., your heart pounding wildly, wondering if you're having an anxiety attack, a massive heart attack or indigestion from the enchiladas suizas you chowed down at dinner? Wouldn't it be nice not to have to leave the comfort of your bed to find out?

Inner Existentialist. Life is meaningless, death is nothingness, you don't exist, so what difference does it make whether you live or die? This archetype can add a little perspective during those 3 a.m. flopsweats—especially when your Inner Internist is scuba diving off St. Bart's.

Inner Groucho Marx. The coyote yuckster himself. Keep him on active duty and you'll never forget that the earth plane is one big wacky Big Top. But stay alert: If you let your Inner Groucho run the show, you may find yourself in a three-way with Cheech and Chong.

Inner Gloria Steinem. A two-in-one deal, your smart, shrewd, independent Inner Gloria mixes firm principles and integrity with inner self-esteem. Just make sure your Inner Groucho is on call in case things get too serious.

Inner Bimbo. She's the shameless lazy nympho sexpot hussy our Inner Gloria says we have to evict from our pantheon once and for all—only she happens to be one of our all-time favorites. Watch out for internecine inner-self warfare as these two archetypal she-babes duke it out.

WORKING WITH YOUR PRECIOUS INNER BEINGS

Now that you've reclaimed your lonely, sawed-off she-selves, why not get down to business and put them to work for you?

Situation. You've been out flexing your primal womanature by trying on hairy pelts at Neiman Marcus. But just as you're about to take an obscenely expensive mink out for a test run, seven rude security guards accost you at the front entrance.

Your Response. Look at them with utter confusion as they rip the hairy pelt from your she-bod, then say in your most demure and apologetic voice: "I'm so sorry, but I had nothing to do with it. It was my Wounded Inner Shoplifter." More than likely, all seven guards are enrolled in twelve-step programs and will weep in empathy and beg you to take the pelt as compensation for your terrible 'childhood.

Situation. You're six months past the deadline for turning in your latest book and you're on page three when your editor calls and asks to see the manuscript.

Your Response. Whisper in French: "Je suis en touch avec mon Inner Flaubert." She'll understand immediately that you, like Flaubert, are a genius and sometimes write only one *mot* a day—but, oh, what a *mot!* In fact, she'll be so awed by your talent and precision with language that she won't disturb you again for several years.

Situation. You're on the dining room table *in delicto flagrante* with Rod, your personal trainer, when your husband arrives home unexpectedly.

Your Response. Smile sweetly and say, "Darling, I'm so happy that you're finally getting to meet my *Inner* Trainer!" If he falls for this, he's really a he-wuss. Buy him a spear and ship him off to the next Iron John Intensive.

Rehabilitating Your Inner Mom

The most amazing thing about your Inner Mom is how much she's like your real mom. This may not come as a total shock, but for those of you who missed out in the mothering department the first time around, learning to give yourself what you didn't get from her—the unconditional love and support of someone who really *likes* you—is no psychosnap. The fact is, no matter how much you'd like to have Mother Earth, Mother Teresa or even Mother Goose starring in your womanpsyche, you're pretty much stuck with you-know-who.

So where does this sorry state of affairs leave a sister who's trying to get whole?

According to Dr. Mildred "Mommie Dearest" Pierce, you're doomed to endlessly repeat your rotten childhood unless you grab your Inner Mom by the inner hand and enroll her in the Betty Ford Clinic of your mind.

STEP ONE: HOW THINGS ARE

This step *is* a psychosnap, because there's absolutely nothing to do. In fact, your entire life up until this minute has been Step One, as is obvious in the following telephone conversation with your real mother—including biting commentary from your Inner Mom.

Real Mom: So? What's new?
Inner Mom: Been out on a date lately?
You: Uh . . .

Real Mom: Really? You're seeing someone?
Inner Mom: You mean there's actually some poor shlub who's interested in *you?*
You: Sort of . . .

Real Mom: Isn't that nice?
Inner Mom: I hope it's a *man.*
You: Yeah, I guess . . .

Real Mom: So what does he do?
Inner Mom: He probably has a prison record like the last one.
You: He's an animal podiatrist . . .

Real Mom: A what?
Inner Mom: Oh well, I suppose that's the only kind of doctor *she* could get. At least he's a *man . . .*
You: I told you. He removes corns and bunions from household pets.

Real Mom: Isn't that nice?
Inner Mom: What difference does it make what he does? It's not going to last anyway.
You: I don't really want to talk about it, okay? It's not going to last anyway.

STEP TWO: AWARENESS

Now that you've caught a little glimpse of how your Inner Mom sabotages your every move even more than your real mom, you have to become even *more* aware of her. *Painfully* aware. The deal here is to bring the whole miserable mess into the harsh fluorescent light of consciousness.

Real Mom: So? How's life? Learn anything new lately?

Inner Mom: What horrible things did your shrink say about me this week?

You: Oh, I don't know. You know . . . (*Noting Inner Mom's total paranoia*)

Real Mom: So, you still in therapy?

Inner Mom: You pathetic, sniveling, hypersensitive mound of protoplasm, who ever heard of so much therapy? Get a grip already.

You: Yes. I'm still in therapy. I told you I was three days ago. (*Feeling Inner Mom's harsh judgments, your eyes well up with tears*)

Real Mom: And? You're making progress?

Inner Mom: You're never going to get better, so you might as well spend your money on some decent clothes instead of sending that mother-bashing charlatan's snot-nosed brats to summer camp.

You: (*Weeping*) Oh . . .

Real Mom: Now, what's the matter? Aren't you getting enough sleep? Have you eaten anything today?

Inner Mom: Not that you couldn't do without a few meals, you disgusting, overweight she-slob. You're probably sleeping fourteen hours a day, too.

You:	I have to go now. (*Hanging up and banging your head against the floorboards*)

That's it. Feel your pain. Beat your breasts. Experience how utterly worthless and despicable *you* think you are. Compared to what you do to yourself, your real mother *is* Mother Teresa. It's a miracle you're still alive.

STEP THREE: HEALING THE MOTHERWOUND

Now that you're in touch with your festering motherwound, it's time to hop up on the old inner delivery table and give birth to a New Inner Mom. An Inner Mom who will love and respect you. An Inner Mom who will bring you ice cream and *not* make you feel like a lowly criminal for eating it.

But, warns Dr. Mildred "Mammy" Pierce, it takes time to work your New Inner Mom into the act. And if you're expecting her to send your old Inner Mom packing, forget it. The best you can hope for is to neutralize her.

The following scene takes place years later. Many things have changed: You're married. You have a child. And now, instead of summer camp, you're putting your shrink's snot-nosed brats through graduate school.

Real Mom:	So? How's little Jason?
Inner Mom:	You spoil that kid rotten. What a mama's boy. I could vomit.
New Inner Mom:	You're a wonderful mother. She's just jealous because *your* child likes you.
You:	(*Having trouble remembering who said what*) Uh, what did you say?
Real Mom:	And that husband of yours? How are you treating him?

Meeting Your Inner Moms

Inner Mom: Who would have believed that such a fine man would have ever married *you?*

New Inner Mom: Fine man, my archetypal ass! You deserve someone who worships the ground you walk on and honors your magnificent womynsoul.

You: Oh, Barney's okay. It's me that's exhausted. (*Big mistake: never, ever volunteer information*)

Real Mom: What do you have to be so exhausted about?

Inner Mom: You lazy slob. You're certainly not tired from housework. Or teaching Inner Chakra EcoAstrology. You call that a *job?*

New Inner Mom: You're contributing to the healing of the planet. The goddess loves you. Ho!

You: I have to go lie down now. (*Fearing multiple personality disorder, you collapse in a heap*)

Honoring Your Real Mom

Because everything in your life has been a reaction to her narcissistic ways, it's possible that in rejecting her, you deprived yourself of her sacred motherwisdom, such as, "As you grow older, go lighter." You may even discover that she mastered some skills you wouldn't mind having yourself:

- sending food back in restaurants without apologizing
- sending it back a second time without apologizing, then insisting on moving to a better table
- saying no to sex and yes to expensive jewelry—all in the same evening
- saying yes to household help and not scouring the place before they get there
- demanding to see the manager in all venues, including flea markets and sidewalk vendor concerns
- saying yes to hair dye, nail polish, makeup, wax, liposuction and all those other little nip-and-tuck procedures without feeling like you're dealing a major blow to Mother Nature.

Tough Love

If wholeness is a multizillion-dollar industry put on by the weekend people, then the inner child is the biggest psychoracket of all time. Think about it. Do you really need to pay some earnest, sweaty guy hundreds of dollars to teach you how to pout, stamp your feet, daydream, whine, squeal, shriek and sob uncontrollably? Have you ever forgotten for even one second how to do these things? Of course not. The fact is, every womansister I've ever met is downright gifted—if not an actual genius—at expressing her inner child. Which, when you get right down to it, is a lot like honoring her mood swings.

As far as I can tell, inner child weekends are really excuses for people to act like big babies in public and get hugged for it. Where else can a grownup who's not a member of a professional ball team score so many points for behaving like a two-year-old? Where else besides Hollywood can the person who throws the biggest tantrum, wails the loudest and maybe even pukes a little become an overnight star?

Did you hear the story—reported in the *New York Times*—about the woman who began sobbing uncontrollably when she learned that the restaurant where she was dining was out of her favorite dessert? "My inner child is really angry that you're out of the gingerbread," she wailed to the waiter. He was speechless, but her dinner companion was not. "That's all right, dear, express you feelings," said the friend. "Even small losses must be mourned."

No two ways about it, most inner children are crying out for tough love. What they really need are weekends that put them in touch with their inner *adult*.

Can't you just picture it? Hotel ballrooms filled with friendly folks in cardigans playing bridge and tittering, saying things like, "Please pass the margarine, Mrs. Winklehoffer" and "Isn't the Creamed Chipped Boeuf tasty tonight?" No one would give testimony about the trauma of discovering that their parents did it. Or *didn't* do it. Or did it with a medley of winter vegetables.

A whole new world of workshop possibilities would open up. Think of the megadollars to be made with seminars like:

- Knitting on the Right Side of the Brain
- Zen and the Art of Flossing
- Insurance Warrior
- Lowering Your Expectations While Increasing Your Bran Intake
- The Way of the Gastroenterologist
- Creating Your Sacred Tax Shelter

Of course, nobody would ever sign up for inner adult weekends because, without all that fun, rowdy, cathartic stuff, you might as well stay home and doze off in front of the TV.

YOUR OUTER CHILD MEETS YOUR INNER CHILD

Now that we're clear on the inner child, there's another little matter to attend to: the outer child. Many parents get their real child mixed up with their inner child, which leads to all sorts of confusion—especially when your actual child is more mature than your inner child or, as is frequently the case, your child's inner child makes your inner child seem like a zygote.

Here are some examples of how this works.

Situation. You live in Texas, where the only life form more sacred than a cheerleader is a side of beef. You're worried that your daughter won't make the cheerleading squad, but her stuck-up rival will. What to do? Console your child or arrange to have her rival bumped off by a sympathetic thug?

What's Really Happening. Neither you nor your inner child ever got close to making the cheerleading squad. The truth is, even though you're resigned to being a housewife, your inner child never gave up her dream of waving a baton and sporting pom-poms. She's the one who's obsessed and plot-

Disciplining Your Inner Child

ting murder. Call your attorney immediately and suggest a "my-inner-child-did-it" defense.

Situation. Your nine-year-old son's gerbil is suddenly stricken with a rare rodent fever and dies. Your son takes the loss of his pet in stride, but you break down at the funeral and are forced to take to your bed.

What's Really Happening. This is an obvious case of mistaken identity—mistaken *species* identity, that is. Instead of identifying with either your inner child or your child's inner child, you're obviously in touch with your inner gerbil and

no amount of reason can convince you that you're not in immediate danger of being struck down by rodent fever too.

Situation. Recently widowed, you hang around your castle until one day this young stud shows up and marries you. You settle into domestic bliss and have a couple of kids before you realize that not only did your new husband kill your old husband (who, coincidentally, happened to be his father), he's also your long-lost son (who you abandoned at birth) *and*—to make matters even worse—you're the mother of your grandchildren. Unable to cope with your family tree, you hang yourself from it.

What's Really Happening. Neither your son, Oed (pronounced "Ed"), nor his inner child has ever forgiven you for abandoning them at birth. What kind of mother are you anyway? How can you possibly mother your own inner child after dumping a helpless infant? And now, not only are your inner child and your outer child disgusted with you, your inner grandchildren hate you too. The only one who still loves you is your inner attorney, who thinks you should sue Oed for mental damages. But Oed's gone and poked his eyes out and it's doubtful that you'll ever collect, so you off

Killing the Inner Nazi

Once upon a womantime, many eons ago or possibly just last week, there was a she-babe named Sheila who was having a bad day. It all started when she woke up and saw that her face was covered with unsightly red splotches. "Oh, no," she cried into her looking glass. "This cannot be! I have a date tonight with a frog!" (Poor Sheila met so few men that she had agreed to go salsa dancing with an amphibian, hoping that if she kissed his slimy lips, he would turn into a handsome prince or—worst-case scenario—Prince.) And though you may wonder why she even cared, since no matter how bad her skin was, the frog's was sure to be worse, Sheila fell to her knees and prayed to Queen Estee, goddess of good skin.

Unfortunately, Queen Estee must have been off creating sacred anti-wrinkle emollients, because Sheila's day went from bad to worse. Not only was her face a mottled mess, she could barely squeeze into her special slinky date dress. (She wasn't sure if this was because she was retaining water or because she'd filled out a little since her last date, five thousand years earlier.) But somehow she

*managed to endure the pre-date plagues that were visited upon her,
including intestinal eruptions that rivalled Vesuvius and insulting
phone calls from her mother. ("What do you mean, a* frog?") *Still,
nothing could dim her womanspirit. But when she arrived at the
Salsa Palace, the little croaker was nowhere to be found. Sheila
searched high and low—especially low—concerned that some insensitive anthropocentric klutz might have stepped on him. At last,
ready to give up, she spied him across the crowded ballroom. But
just as she was about to call his name, another womansister—a sister with no splotches on her face, a sister whose slinky date dress did
not look three sizes too small—bent down and kissed him. Within
seconds, the frog turned into a man.*

*Sheila began to shriek and pull her hair out, but the former frog—
who looked more like an overworked accountant with a passion for poly-
ester than either a prince or Prince—didn't even recognize her. She col-
lapsed on the dance floor in a seething, snarling, hysterical heap.*

*The room quickly emptied, except for a pale young man in a
toga. He leaned over and put his mouth right next to Sheila's ear.
"All is love," he whispered. "Just think positive, joyful thoughts.
You create your own reality." Her moans grew even louder. She tried
to bite his ear off.*

*"I'm going to leave you with one parting gift," the young man
said. "It's an affirmation. Repeat after me: 'I am a happy, joyous
being. I feel no pain. My life is absolutely perfect.'"*

*With that, Sheila picked herself up off the dance floor, ran out
of the ballroom, down the steps of the Salsa Palace, out into the
darkness and into the nearest swamp, never to be seen again.*

But sometimes on summer nights, when the air is thick with
ribets, *you can still hear Sheila's shrieks, rising from the deep.*

"Gimme a break, La Poodela!" I hear you groan. "You're
breaking all your own rules. How can we possibly place our
trust in a sister who pulls the rug out from under our sacred
heels? I thought you *hated* fairy tales!"

But that's just the point. The beauty part of being a

poodlewoman and an *essential* teaching of my anti-self-improvement program: You don't have to be consistent! You're entitled to change your womanmind!

Because the day may come when you too need a fairy tale to shriek your truth.

That day may be sooner than you think.

So slip into a pair of high heels and listen up.

Because it takes a tale of mega mythopoeic dimensions to describe the most fearsome, most dangerous, most heinous and hateful inner self there is.

I am speaking of the Inner Nazi.

This is the tyrant who says that *on some deep level,* you *wanted* to get caught between two warring sumo wrestlers or have your husband leave you for his AA sponsor.

The Inner Nazi is chief of the Think-Positive Police.

The Inner Nazi is head of the You-Create-Your-Own-Reality Firing Squad.

The Inner Nazi is the creep who scares you into thinking you're going to give yourself cancer if you feel depressed or a heart attack if you get pissed off.

The Inner Nazi whispers in mellow and beatific tones that life would be a total groove if you just got with the program and visualized yourself on a white sandy beach. (Apparently, the Inner Nazi hasn't heard the news about skin cancer.)

The Inner Nazi is the archetype who was the architect of poor Sheila's tragic and untimely death.

Because if Sheila had been allowed to throw her womanfit in peace, she would have eventually gotten over it. She never would have drowned herself in the dark and icy swamp. She would have gone to Miami Beach instead.

As if feeling miserable isn't bad enough, *the Inner Nazi makes you feel miserable about feeling miserable.*

(Sometimes the Inner Nazi sounds a lot like your mother.)

A POP QUIZ

Here's a little quizette to help you find out who's really running the show: you or your Inner Nazi.

1. When the World Trade Center blew up, did you think

    a. you were personally responsible because of your negative vibes, even though you were in Kazakhstan at the time?

    b. the employees inside the towers must have unconsciously wanted to leave work early?

    c. terrorists had something to do with it?

2. When Mel Gibson got married, did you

    a. feel really bummed and rejected because you knew that if only you had visualized yourself married to Mel, today *you* would be the much-envied Mrs. G?

    b. think the reason he didn't marry any of your friends either is because they're lousy at visualizing too?

    c. consider that one reason why Mel married the woman he did was because he had actually met her?

3. If you're flat broke and on the verge of downsizing your living quarters from a ranch house to a cardboard box, do you think it's because

    a. on some deep level you're not ready to receive the prosperity of the universe?

    b. your dysfunctional parents really hated you, otherwise they would have left you a seven-figure trust fund and you wouldn't be in this mess?

    c. you got laid off three years ago and haven't been able to find another job since?

4. If your doctor told you that you were anemic, would you

a. try to understand why on some deep level you choose to empower your white blood cells more than your red?

b. blame your dysfunctional parents for making you eat overcooked vegetables during your miserable, rotten childhood?

c. take iron tablets and eat a lot of spinach?

5. If you order a glass of chardonnay in a restaurant, do you

a. see the glass as half-empty, but blame it on your pessimistic outlook?

b. see the glass as half-empty and scream at the bartender for stiffing you?

c. see a clear vessel filled to the halfway mark with overpriced fermented grape juice?

If you answered (c) to one or more questions, congratulations! Your Inner Nazi has been disarmed. If you answered (b) to one or more questions, your Inner Nazi is completely paranoid and out of control, but will never admit it, so you might as well give up right now. If you answered (a) to even one question, you are a pathetic New Age victim who desperately needs this book! Your Inner Nazi has just started World War III and *the enemy is you!*

Lite Thoughts

Maybe I'm a person of differing cerebro-luminosity (dimwit), but I just don't get this whole affirmation business.

Like why, if you're fat and sad and suicidal, would you walk around all day saying, "My zest for life is reflected in my joyful and abundant presence" instead of going to a shrink and maybe step class?

Not only does pretending you're a joyous being *not* make you one, it makes you a liar too. Or—at the very least—it puts you in denial, which is bad, right?

Like, how are you supposed to heal your womanpain if you pretend you don't have any?

Does anyone honestly think that a nice affirmation or two would have taken the heat off Joan of Arc?

What if Dracula, Medea and a few other discarnate celebrities went into recovery? Would they be warmly received? Would Hitler be embraced as the adult child of a severely dysfunctional family? (Classic case of perfectionism!) What affirmations could have helped these folks get whole?

Dracula	"I nourish myself with love. I digest life with ease."
Lady Macbeth	"I release today and slip into peaceful sleep, trusting that tomorrow and tomorrow and tomorrow will take care of itself."
Elvis	"I live in the now. I deserve to be alive."
Joan of Arc	"I gravitate toward warmth. I'm always in the right place at the right time."
Jack the Ripper	"It is my birthright to have my needs met. I rejoice in my masculinity."
Anne Boleyn	"I have a good head on my shoulders. Those closest to me love and appreciate me for who I am."
Prometheus	"Life is effortless. My burden is light."
Queen Victoria	"I am at home in my body. I rejoice in my sexuality."
Ivan the Terrible	"I release the past. All is forgiven and forgotten. I love and approve of me."
Gertrude Stein	"A platitude is a platitude is a platitude . . ."

The Shadow _Doesn't_ Always Know

People often ask me, hey, La Poodela, what about my shadow? Where's the best place to meet it? Should I use a matchmaker? Take out a personals ad? How will I know it's _my_ dark side and not somebody else's?

These and other life-and-death questions are plaguing weekend workshop survivors who've been instructed to embrace their shadow—all the hideous pain and rage locked away in the attic of their beingness—in order to get whole. This has led to mass confusion and hysteria.

Take the sad case of Natasha Greenblatt of Oil City, Pennsylvania. "Before I got in touch with my shadow, I was famous from one end of Oil City to the other for my sunny disposition and my sublime noodle kugel," Greenblatt recalls wistfully. "But now, I'm depressed and miserable all the time. I can't stop crying or beating the furniture and, ever since that little episode at the temple bake sale when I honored my rage by sending a dozen lemon meringue pies airborne, people run like the dickens when they see me coming."

The tragedy is, Natasha is not alone. All across the earth plane, millions of innocent wholeness seekers have embraced

L L. Cool Poodela

their dark side only to discover that, once held, the shadow clings and squeals and refuses to let go.

THE SHADOW RAP

If I'm acting bad and that doesn't mean good
doin' nothin at all the way a she-babe should
don't look at me, don't diss what I do
'cause it ain't me, babe, it's my shadow
  shadow shadow shadow
That ice archetype from Mister Jung
makes you sweat all over covers you like a
rug all that darkness misery demon-lovin' pain
you're as strung out as some basehead blitzed on cocaine
Now listen up know what I'm sayin'
you can wail and holler and weep and start flayin'
yourself if you mean to but that's not all
so get a grip get stupid get large and in charge
  of your shadow shadow shadow shadow
Yo, it's my mission don't need your
permission to break it down give you the flavor
how much pain do you need to savor?
The merchants of darkness are everywhere
fattening their calves on your despair
So take it light but don't be nice
it's just your soul on sale for a price
by hungry vendors dressed up like saints
selling what's yours feeding off your complaints
You got to own it to hone it, chance to dance
  with your shadow shadow shadow shadow

Ten Signs You're _Not_ Codependent

You may be shocked to discover that you are _not_ among the traumatized 96% of Americans diagnosed by "experts" as codependent or—if you've done your grief work—_codependent no more_. Then again, you may be in complete and utter denial—in which case, you should enter recovery as soon as possible, just as soon as you figure out what it is you're supposed to be recovering from.

Still, there's a slim chance you fall into that tiny 4% minority who are _codependent not now, not ever_—but only if you exhibit the following tendencies.

1. You think that being shamed by your toxic parents is _not_ necessarily the traumatic equivalent of being held as a political prisoner or tortured by terrorists.

2. You don't feel a burning desire to do your "grief work" on national television.

3. You're not absolutely sure what your grief work is,

but you trust that when the time comes you'll know what to do.

4. You know the last names of your most intimate friends.

5. You don't feel compelled to nurture the green fuzz growing inside your refrigerator, even though it's a living microecosystem put there by your Higher Power.

6. You hate cats: the pet, the musical, the product tie-ins.

7. Given the choice between spending your free time owning your pain or a house in the country, you'd choose the latter.

8. You would like to believe that wholeness can be achieved *without* destroying the English language, as in: "I can't take out the garbage right now, I'm journaling."

9. You believe that a little interdependence among living beings is not such a bad thing. Come to think of it, a little denial comes in mighty handy too.

10. You dream of being a woman who runs with the Woolfs: Leonard and Virginia.

Once you've established that you're merely neurotic—not codependent, not dysfunctional, not a sick and desperate shopaholic who craves sparkly costume jewelry—you may feel a deep urge to form a support group, since there are so few plain old neurotics left.

Try to stifle this urge.

Part Two

Poodle Nation

Putting on the Dog

Yoohoo, womansisters, now listen up.

You've come a long way. You've learned to shriek your truth to anyone who'll listen and *everyone* who won't. You're partial and proud. So far so good. But don't let it go to your womanhead, because it's still too soon to send out invitations to your Heeled-Into-Wholeness Ritual Celebration Ball. That's right. We're not home yet.

Because there's a little something we haven't tackled yet.

You know what it is, don't you?

The time has come to face the biggest challenge of your anti-self-improvement program: daring to be imperfect where it really hurts—your she-looks.

So drop everything, strap on your favorite heels and get ready to run with the women who run with Naomi Wolf.

GIRLSTUFF

I don't know about you, but I was born without the girl gene. No matter how hard I try, I can't seem to pull together a look that doesn't include several embarrassing defects in both my person and my ensemble, such as

- dried, caked foodstuffs
- bits o' flora
- over-the-hill footwear
- safety pins and—on special occasions—staples
- fur and dander belonging to non-human members of the animal kingdom
- hair of indescribable shape and hue

By now, you've probably checked out the photograph to see if I really look like the stapled-together she-slob dripping with last night's linguini that I just described. But that's the amazing part: To look at me, you'd think I was a regular womansister, tripping and breaking her heel on life's highway. It's only upon closer inspection that you can see I'm a *complete and total wreck.*

This used to cause me unspeakable shame. Ever since I was a wee inner child, I suffered from mental anguish due to my lack of girlstuff know-how. I liked pink okay, but I was always falling down in the dirt. And, more than once, the elastic on my panties expired right in the middle of jumping rope. As I grew older, my shame deepened, but there was nowhere to turn. No support groups. No hotlines or relevant fairy tales to help me get to the root of my Not-A-Real-Girl complex. In fact, until I began "Heeling Into Wholeness" (mismatched and broken heels welcome), I thought I was the only one. A lone misfit among the perfectly turned out. My secret shame drove me to become a writer: It's the only profession where no one *cares* whether you merge with your Inner Donna Karan, because nobody ever actually *sees* you.

Imagine my shock and delight to discover that the only people in the whole world who really have the girl thing down are Ivana Trump, Charo, my mother and certain female impersonators.

Do you think I want to look like *them?*

Every week I receive *thousands* of letters from grateful, out-of-the-closet-and-proud poodleslob survivors from around the globe.

DEAR LA POODELA,
Last night at a chic, high-society do, I was halfway through my Veal Oscar (the other half was conveniently resting on my bosom) before I realized that I was wearing my panty hose *over* my little black dress. In the past I would have shrieked in horror and relocated immediately to Paraguay. But this time, with you as my inspiration, I hopped up on the table and rumbaed the night away!

Thank you! Merci! Toda raba!

"DARING TO BE IMPERFECT ON
CENTRAL PARK SOUTH"

YO! LIKE LA POODELA!
We're like, ho! We're like, whoa! We like owe you everything!

DARLENE AND TIFFANY
("THE GRUNGE SISTERS")
SEATTLE, WASHINGTON

DEAR MS. LA POODELA,
Right after I saw you on "Goodmorning, Ohio!" decked out in your pink chenille bathrobe, high heels and many charming hats, I ripped my drab business

suit from my she-flesh and proceeded to put on the *entire* contents of my closet. I sensed a whole new life unfolding!

I was right. When I got to the building where I work, I stood in the lobby shrieking "Ethel shmethyl merman ho!" Oh, La Poodela, I felt so empowered! So free— just like you said. Unfortunately, the feeling didn't last long, because before I knew it, five burly policemen had me pinned to the elevator and were slapping handcuffs around my wrists.

Please, La Poodela, help! Is there a defense fund for women who have been institutionalized for honoring their mood swings through fashion?

"PAM" T.
THE CHER RECOVERY CENTER
YOUNGSTOWN, OHIO

YOGAWOMAN GOES SOHO

Once you've made peace with the fact that you're *never* going to get the girl thing straight, you might as well give up trying to find that one look that screams *you!* Because even though in dark and troubled herstory days gone by, you had to pick your look and stick to it, with my unique Poodle-woman Mix-And-Match Liberation Plan, you can say good-bye to rigid old stereotypes and bonjour to chaos! Now you can choose a style to match your mood swings. (With any luck, you won't end up like poor "Pam" T.)

Here are some contemporary looks for you to choose from. Don't hesitate to try them all—at once! They *all* scream you!

Hermeswoman. The regulation everything: Hermes scarf, Ferragamo bag, Chanel suit, Manolo Blahnik shoes, Fendi sunglasses, Louis Vuitton luggage. Hermeswoman is a general in the Euro-Gucci-Armani army. Habitat: Upper East Side and adjoining suburbs—Greenwich, Palm Beach, Beverly Hills, Aspen, Montecatini de Terme. Refrigerator contents: arugula, Evian water, champagne, Godiva chocolates. Favorite role model: herself, *naturellement.*

Hermeswoman

Faux Hermeswoman

Faux Hermeswoman. Wears all of the above, also purchased on Fifth Avenue—only from sidewalk vendors. This she-babe sneaks around in a wig and dark glasses so no one catches her buying fifteen-dollar Rolex watches or Louis Vuitton de Taiwan luggage. Lochmann's is her Lourdes. Lives in West Palm Beach and its suburbs: Fort Lauderdale, Fort Lee, Forest Hills, Short Hills, Tel Aviv. Refrigerator contents: rugelach, seltzer, Milk of Magnesia, Milky Ways.

Winnebagowoman. This she-gal loves wash n' wear wear that is casual, affordable and comes in every color of the rainbow—and then some. She's especially fond of rubber and petroleum-based fabrics—ideal for those endless road trips to historic shopping complexes, where the stores have cute names like Ye Olde Tchochtke Shoppe. Favorite movie: *Lost In America.*

Winnebagowoman

Yogawoman

Yogawoman. Wears only loose-fitting garments made from natural fibers and holistic dyes—perfect for mythic-Inca-ritual-high-colonic-and-astral-aikido weekends. Occupation: shiatsu-dreambody-and-ecstatic-inner-dance acutherapist. Favorite punctuation mark: the hyphen. Refrigerator contents: tofu, tempeh, hijiki, acidophilus, and wheat grass shakes for those hard-to-satisfy cravings. Heartthrobs: Ramtha, Seth, E.T.

Sohowoman. For this serioso babe, getting dressed is a snap: black, black and more black—with the occasional two-hundred-dollar white cotton T-shirt thrown in for variety and self-expression. Note: there's a slim chance that Sohowoman's lack of imagination is due to the fact that she only shops in stores with nine items or less. Her credo: life is art, art is life, fashion is a two-legged psychopolitical moving installation. Major life problem: being mistaken for a wait-person in downtown eating establishments.

Sohowoman

Slothwoman

Slothwoman. (My personal favorite.) This distracted sister doesn't so much choose her clothes as they choose her. When dressing in the morning (*if* she gets that far), she's likely to select her ensemble from the mountain of clothes on top of her stationary bicycle. Chances are, the outfit has not been freshly laundered. Best friend: proprietor of nearest Szechuan take-out establishment. Favorite spiritual practice: The Poodlewoman Out-Of-Body Experience (napping).

UpToTheMinutewoman. Unlike "Daring to be Imperfect on Central Park South," this fashion lemming *deliberately* wears her underwear on the outside—or was that last season? She's grunge, she's plaid, she's chiffon-and-macrame. Major life questions: to tattoo or not to tattoo? The pros and cons of nostril jewelry? How bell her bottoms? Psychiatric diagnosis: hemline anxiety disorder. Man of dreams? Just a minute, she's checking.

UpToThe Minute Woman

Shtetlwoman

Shtetlwoman. Famous for introducing the layered look to the New World, Shtetlwoman hails from Pinsk by way of Great Neck. Though she exhibits a strong Indo-Afro–Mayan-Hopi influence, her love of long flowing skirts, babushkas, beads and giant dangling earrings is balanced by her unwavering commitment to sensible footwear. Favorite colors: purple, violet, plum, lavender, grape, lilac, magenta. Role models: Gypsy Rose Lee, Pocahontas and her great-aunt Belle of Bialystock.

LLBeanwoman. This no-nonsense trekker hasn't set foot in a store since making the most important discovery of her womanlife: catalogues. Amazing fact: she's too busy rigging masts and sharpening her survival skills to notice that she's missing the girlstuff gene or that her mail-order frocks don't fit. Refrigerator contents: beef jerky, trail mix, freeze-dried moose n' spinach spread. Role models: Paul Bunyan, Annie Oakley, the Donner Party.

LLBeanwoman

Creating Your Sacred Space: The Poodlewoman Closet

An essential step of my no-step heeling program is to create your own sacred space. In this case, you'll want to know where and how to store your heels. And, if you fully embrace my Poodlewoman Mix-and-Match Liberation Plan, you may find that you require *several* sacred spaces. Try to arrange for at least one of the walk-in variety, with a full-length mirror, so you'll have a safe place in which to conduct sacred try-on–tear-off–stamp-your-feet-and-weep-uncontrollably rituals.

Empowerment Through Accessories

This sounds like a good idea. A fabulous idea. Only I have absolutely nothing to say on the subject because, in addition to lacking the girl gene, I am accessory-impaired—or, rather, in these PC times—accessory challenged.

I lose them. I break them. I don't know what to do with them. The truth is, beyond the obvious scarf, belt and bauble triad, I don't even know what they are. Every day, I see armies of womansisters marching down the streets of our nation with all sorts of unrecognizable items pinned to their clothing, dangling from every inch of their beings. What are these things? Where do they get them?

Please. Don't tell me.

Because there's also the problem of figuring out what goes with what. Or what sort of accessory items, *if any*, you like. What if you've outgrown eucalyptus pod necklaces, but you don't really see yourself as Tiffanywoman? And what about the issue of taste? As far as I can tell, practically all

Empowerment Through Accessories

accessories—even the really expensive ones, which, if you ask me, are not that easily distinguished from the K-Mart variety—are ugly but nobody has the guts to say so. It's like this giant conspiracy by the home shopping network and novelty merchants to hoodwink innocent women and make them junk themselves up like berserk Christmas trees.

Well, I'm here to tell you that you look better *without* them.

For those of you who still cling to the belief that accessories are what separate us from the animals, hey, I'm sorry, but you're on your own.

The Tree-Falls-in-the-Forest School of Personal Grooming

Since the dawn of my adolescence, heralded by the forestation of my legs, armpits and *down there,* I've been wrestling with the body-hair question. For one thing, I'm dark and hairy. I'm also lazy and easily bored. And, except in rare, kinky moments, I'm no great fan of blood or pain. Unfortunately, most hair-removal activities—depending on your method—are painful, bloody, time consuming and a total snooze. This doesn't even take into account the whole infuriating entropy issue: *The minute you slash it, it starts to grow back.*

So, why bother, you ask? Why not follow the lead of our pioneer womansisters of the 1970s and do absolutely nothing? Why not just drop the whole pretense that we're smooth and hairless and rejoice in our womanfur?

I'll tell you why.

Hairy legs look disgusting and make you feel ugly. So do little sleeveless dresses that show off your amazonjungle armpits.

There. I said it.

I used to think I'd been brainwashed by whitepigmale Euro-mindcontrol techniques. I refused to wax, shave or depilitorize. And I held firm to the belief that any she-person who did was a pathetic, self-hating womantraitor. Then came the revelation:

I hate my hairy legs and pits more than men do.

Unfortunately, the revelation has done nothing to solve the disgusting, never-ending problem of hair removal. Which is where my Tree-Falls-In-The-Forest School of Personal Grooming fits right in.

If no one sees it, you don't have to:

- shave it
- wax it
- buff or polish it
- trim it
- bleach it
- shape it
- tweeze it
- epilady it

If someone *does* see it, but that someone has lived with you for at least five years (two years, if you're over forty) or is under four feet tall, the tree-falls-in-the-forest rule can be suspended at whim.

And, next January when you start whining about the weather, remember that winter—that much-maligned season—is the hirsute poodlesister's best friend!

Why do you think so many dark-haired wimmin live in the Northeast?

Tonsorial Tsuris

While we're on the subject, the stuff growing out of the top of your head is a whole other ball o'wax. Here, unless you're Sinead O'Connor, you want lots of it, you want people to see it but, most of all, you want it to look good.

Why?

Because more than any other part of the female anatomy, a woman identifies with her hair. A woman *is* her hair. In fact, it's very hard to have a really bad hair day, but a good day otherwise. Because for some crazy reason that scientists have yet to explain, the hairdo is directly linked to the she-babe soul.

Think about it. When did you ever get together with your mother or your friends and not immediately launch into a three-hour discussion of everybody's hair—even when you spent *less* than three hours together?

The thing is, everybody (except poodles) hates their hair. It's either too frizzy, thin, thick, limp, dull, stringy or bears an uncanny resemblance to poorly pruned shrubbery. Or maybe it has a mind of its own. (I'll let you in on a little secret: everyone's hair has a mind of its own. Where do you think the term *hairbrain* comes from?)

Then there's the color nightmare, which is an entire subcategory in itself. All I'll say on this subject is that *most* of the people walking around with pink, purple or bright orange hair did not deliberately choose those color options. The same cannot be said of bad haircuts. Many people seem to love a bad haircut. Don't ask me why. All I know is that an alarmingly high number of them show up on daytime TV talk shows.

Can This Hair Day Be Saved?

Okay, so I know what you're thinking: Here it comes, the pitch, the program, the workshop. "Making Love To Your Inner Follicle." Well, you've got it all wrong. Because La Poodela is not one of those quick-fix, "C'mon down to the holistic beauty parlor and we'll heal it on the weekend" types of prophet or guru. Nosiree, Gladys. No way am I going to tell you to love your hair.

I'm going to tell you to hate your hair.

Because you already do.

You can take it from there.

Hi, My Name Is La Poodela...

Hi, my name is La Poodela and I have a confession to make. A deep dark secret that fills me with shame.

I can't live without food.

You heard me.

I'm going to say it out loud, again and again, until the day comes when I can say it with love and forgiveness.

Hi, my name is La Poodela and I'm an eataholic.

That's right.

The truth is, even though I try to take things one day at a time, I can barely make it through a morning—let alone an entire day—without a fix.

Pathetic, huh?

I crave the stuff. It's a physical thing. When I don't get any I feel a gnawing pain deep within the pit of my being-ness. Before long, I start to feel spacy and then the shaking starts. After that, watch out. It's not a pretty picture, but I can't help it.

They say it's a disease over which I have no control.

They say it's genetic. My whole twisted family is the same way. We can't be in the same room together for even an hour without indulging our habit. I've never told anyone this before, but the codependency between my grandmother and her butcher is terrifying. She can't do *anything* unless there's a dead chicken nearby.

Hi, my name is La Poodela and I'm a slave to my addiction.

I know I eat to fill the emptiness inside. I know food is a substitute for love—but don't get me started, because I'm a total failure in that department too.

It's not that I don't have love in my life. The fact is, I have a wonderful relationship. You'd think that would be enough to get me to kick the habit—and maybe it would be for a normal person—but not me. No, my sickness runs so deep that even true love doesn't stop me from wanting to fill the void.

I'm never satisfied. No matter how well things are going I obsess about being a woman who grills with Wolfgang Puck.

Sometimes I feel like just giving up.

My shrink, Dr. Julia Inner-Child, says I crave food for reasons other than dulling the wounds left over from my painful childhood—like if I *don't* eat I'll die—but I think she's just saying that to make me feel better.

Because if it were true, why would I feel so guilty, like I'm committing murder with every morsel?

But that's not the worst of it.

There's more.

You see, I'm not one of those quiet, no-fuss types who satisfies her cravings without a lot of hullabaloo.

No way. I'm no handful-of-lettuce, popcorn-for-dinner, yogurt-on-the-run type babe who sneaks around and gets stoked when nobody's looking.

I want the primo stuff.

Three times a day. (Maybe it's just a coincidence that poodles are famous for being able to tell a nice piece of filet mignon from el cheapo top round, but I doubt it.)

And—call me an exhibitionist—I don't even mind if people see me get zonked in public.

I am Poodlewoman, watch me chew.

That's right: not only am I powerless over my disease, my feminine side suffers from a serious imbalance too.

Because if I were a *real* woman, I would pick, graze, nibble and con everyone around me into believing that I subsisted on lettuce and Sweet-n'-Low-laced iced tea. Maybe I'd even stick my finger down my throat. What I wouldn't do is sit down in public and brazenly enjoy a hearty meal—a very *Y-chromosome* thing to do.

But even that's not all of it: I never forget to eat either. Terrible things could be happening, the whole country could be going up in smoke, and still I'd wonder what's for lunch.

There's no end to my shame.

I know it's my disease talking, but sometimes I feel like the pusher on the playground. "Come here, little girl, let me show you what's in this baggie . . ." I drag others down with me. I try not to, but sometimes I just can't help myself.

Hi, my name is La Poodela and I'm an eataholic.

Would you like to have dinner with me?

La Poodela's Little Tips for Living on the Earth Plane

Do you ever stop and think, yo!, like what's with the equipment? Why do I get headaches, heartburn, bunions, back pain, postnasal drip, a trick knee, testy intestines and PMS? And that's on a *good* day! A day when you're "in the pink" or, as your internist might decree, "in perfect health."

Confusing, isn't it?

The fact is, life as an incarnate being is a lot like scaling Everest—only it's all downhill. Here are some pointers to help smooth your descent.

1. "Perfect health" is relative. What it really means is that you're not dying of a terminal disease. (Yet.)

2. Feeling "under the weather" is the number-one side

effect of being alive. (However, it should be noted that the real weather is also "under the weather" most of the time—especially in New York City.)

3. For all their elaborate theories and scientific mumbo jumbo, doctors don't really *know* anything. They have more in common with high-stakes gamblers playing the horses at Hialeah than God, and should be treated accordingly.

4. "Mind over body" techniques notwithstanding, your body has the upper hand (in every way!). Your only hope is to shower it with kindness.

5 Ask your significant other if he thinks you're fat. If he says yes, punish him for his insensitivity. If he says no, punish him for lying.

6. Just for fun, visualize a meal in which you experience neither abject guilt nor extreme deprivation with every bite.

7. You can't do it, can you?

8. Techniques meant to make you relax don't. Better you should get in touch with what a tense wreck you are.

9. For mothers who love too much: It's an incurable disease that doesn't improve with time or age—yours or theirs. The best you can do is remember to breathe and go to the movies as often as possible.

10. Avoid out-of-body experiences (unless you have a round-trip ticket). Believe me, it was tricky enough getting into the damn thing in the first place. If you split now, there's no guarantee you'll get back in—which might be construed as passive-aggressive behavior by relatives left behind to deal with you in vegetable form.

11. It's a wonder, isn't it, that after everything life puts them through, so many people are actually up and walking around? It's a wonder that you're up and walking around. Meditate on this at least once a day.

12. For the hypochondriacs in the crowd: When you develop a mysterious new symptom you're sure is lung cancer or a brain tumor, wait one week before having a complete workup or selecting music for your funeral. Chances are the symptoms will either go away or be replaced by the sudden onset of sleeping sickness (even though no tse-tse flies have been sighted in your area since 1938). Warning: The One-Week Rule does not apply if you're running a high fever or are the recent recipient of a gunshot wound.

13. Also for the hypochondriacs: You can stop worrying. You're going to die. On the bright side, once you accept this shocking news, you'll start having more fun.

Nobody's Pet

```
WARNING:
WOMEN WHO RUN WITH THE POODLES
GENERALLY DO NOT EXCEL
IN THE SERVICE PROFESSIONS
```

I'm putting it on the record. I'm shouting it loud and clear.

I am opposed to work.

It's not that I mind working. It's Work I can't handle. The kind where they expect you to show up five mornings in a row—*wearing pantyhose*—then stay *all day.* For *fifty* weeks a year! For around *fifty years!*

Whose life is it, anyway?

What if you wake up with a headache? What if there's a big sale at your favorite French shoe store—which happens

La Poodela's Personal Power Center

to be in Paris? What if you have to take your inner mother to the podiatrist or meet your shadow for a late lunch? What do you do then?

Don't ask me, because I don't have a clue.

Call me jobaphobic. Call me a traitor to wimmin. Call me anything you want, just don't make me go to Work.

I can't help it. I was born this way. It's probably a past-life thing. Maybe I was a slave in Egypt, where they turned you into a mummy before you could shout "mommy" if you didn't punch in at the Pyramids on time.

When I was growing up (this lifetime), my numero-uno role model was Proust, who had the good sense to do his work in bed—with a big stash of cookies on hand at all times. (All things considered, crumbs in the bed is a more desirable occupational hazard than, say, asbestos poisoning or getting yelled at by your boss.)

That's another concept I just don't get: the boss. Like, I'm going to let somebody tell *me* what to do? Who? Why?

It's not that I don't believe passionately in equality in the Workplace—I do! It's just that—personally—I live in terror of ever having to go there.

I can't wait for the day when jobaphobia is recognized as a legitimate disease, like having parents or being addicted to noodles. (You think it's a *coincidence* that the guy in the Old Testament who suffered more than anybody is called *Job?*) Self-help groups will sprout up all over the nation and Oprah will shed real tears when her jobaphobic guests reveal their secret to the American people.

Maybe on that bright new day we won't have to endure our abuse in silence anymore. Maybe jobist pigs will think twice before they taunt us and call us dirty names, like lazy, good-for-nothing, bum, princess and the dirtiest slur of all—*freelance.*

In the meantime, I know I'm not alone.

The truth is, *nobody* wants to go to Work—at least not five days a week, year after year.

Why do you think there are so many writers?

Do you think any of us (except Joyce Carol Oates) really gets off on writing? Of course not. It's a miserable occupation, with endless hours, no money and a lot of built-in grief work. But for most writers, the only thing worse than writing is not writing. And going to a job.

So why doesn't somebody say something?

Well, I'm here to break the ice.

I'm here to tell you that the Protestant Ethic is ruining everybody's life.

I'm here to tell you how you can have it all . . . your way.

A Guide to Having It All . . . Your Way

There are a number of creative ways to get money without having to endure the suffering of Job by going to a job. Here are a few possibilities.

1. Be born into a lot of money. Somebody's got to do it. Why shouldn't *you* be one of those lucky gals who grows up believing that "summer" and "winter" are verbs?

2. Become a professional jobaphobic. Go on Sally Jessy and weep uncontrollably as you publicly own your "disease." Make sure all the big publishers and agents are watching. Insist on Marla Maples for the "Movie of the Week."

3. Become a religious leader. Rent a hall and surround yourself with grinning attendants who fan you as you channel a dead entity with a biblical-sounding name who says deep things like, "Lo, your life on the earth plane is a vast supermarket of possibility. Do not partake only of canned goods."

4. Start your own New Age business. In no other area of commerce will your overhead be so low. Become an out-of-body tour guide, an astral plane pilot, an inner child pediatrician or, if you like wearing a white coat and fooling around in a lab, invent the much-needed rebirth control pill.

5. Become a writer. At your own peril—unless you're one of the lucky ones who has one simplistic, obvious idea and cannot write—in which case, your success is guaranteed.

Reclaiming Your Sacred Inner Bitch: Advanced Training

As with any intimate bond between two beings, you cannot expect your relationship with your Sacred Inner Bitch to thrive unless you spend quality time with her. You've got to love her. Nurture her. Take her out for a romp through the mall or for a surprise visit to the office of Senator Jesse Helms. If you don't, the consequences may be serious, even fatal: You could find yourself apologizing to rude salespeople, eating moldy shrimp, or sending your hairdresser flowers for making it look like you and Willard Scott were separated at birth.

A good way to keep your Sacred Inner Bitch in shape is to write letters to anyone living or dead who ever pissed you off—or who you think *might* piss you off at some future date. (Remember: Entitlement is *not* just for the royals.)

Here are some samples to get the ball rolling.

DEAR DOKTOR FREUD:

Just exactly how do *you* know so much about the female orgasm? I mean, seriously, did you ever have one? Plus, that was a real cute trick you pulled with the seduction theory. Right, like zillions of womansisters *wanted* their fathers, uncles, brothers and shrinks to stick it to them, so they *made it up.* Thanks for believing us, Sig. You really helped boost the self-esteem of wimmin everywhere.

(FOR WOMYNWRITERS ONLY:)
DEAR JOYCE CAROL OATES:

Stop writing so much! You make the rest of us look like total she-slobs. What's with you, anyway? Don't you ever get a headache?

DEAR MOM AND DAD:

I just want to drop you a line to thank you for teaching me to "keep my trap shut" and not to "ruffle any feathers." I'm sure these qualities would have been a real plus in ninth-century Japan. Enclosed please find an invoice for 14 years of analysis, 11 years of karate (plus belts in a wide assortment of colors) and 742 self-esteem workshops.

DEAR MADONNA:

We admire your courage to say what's on your mind but, honestly, enough already with those breasts! You're not the only woman on the planet to own a pair and, frankly, they're just not *that* interesting.

DEAR FASHION MAGAZINE EDITORS OF AMERICA:

Come off it! The new shapely and voluptuous womyn is a *size six?* Right, and I'm Marie Antoinette (who's been sadly misunderstood for centuries all because she offered the people of Paris a fattening confection!). Who do you think reads your stupid magazines, anyhow? Famine victims?

DEAR ARNOLD SCHWARZENEGGER:

Sorry, Arnie, but biceps the size of bowling balls are *not* a turn-on. What the American people need now is a hero with a little strategically placed flab.

TO ALL THE MEN WHO EVER LIVED:

We confess. We're the original oppressor. We admit that back in old Minos, around thirty thousand years ago (give or take a millennium), we shamelessly used you to make babies, then sliced and diced you into little pieces and *spritzed* our crops with your blood. (Ironic, isn't it, how *you* were the symbol of fertility back then!) Okay, okay, so we didn't just use you as fertilizer, we ate your raw flesh (*homme tartare!*) for dinner too. But, hey, that was a *long* time ago—so *get over it.* You've more than evened the score.

DEAR SHANNEN DOHERTY:

Not to worry, doll: *Your* Sacred Inner Bitch is operating at full capacity.

Finding a Femtor

Men have mentors. Wimmin need femtors. In these confusing times, we all deserve a helping hand. And since those who've already passed on can teach us their tricks without having to worry that we're going to steal their thunder or get better reviews, it's best to choose a femtor from the spirit world.

But before you do, could somebody please explain how, if everybody's reincarnating all the time, they can come back to earth and take on new bodies *while* simultaneously remaining on call in the Great Beyond? I mean, if you're pretty sure your two-year-old used to be your grandfather, how is it that you can contact him in a seance too? Do our spirits subdivide endlessly like hideous housing tracts or what?

Of course you can't explain this. But don't feel bad, because nobody, not even high-priced psychics or gurus, can.

Here, then, are several candidates for femtor from the exclusive Poodlewoman Pantheon.

The Women of Troy put an end to the Trojans' shameless pursuit of that hussy Helen by setting their ships on fire. Afterward, they ravished the boys with kisses and apologized for such a thoughtless act.

Aretaphila of Cyrene rid her city of tyrants, then spent the rest of her days doing needlepoint.

After three miserable marriages to unfaithful brutes, **Zoe, Empress of Byzantium,** gave up and became pious and virginal again. (Obviously, she was the femtor of **Doris Day** who, after two failed marriages, reincarnated herself as the Virgin of Hollywood.)

Godiva, often misunderstood as a flasher instead of a she-ro, rode naked through the streets of Coventry in 1040 after her husband Ceofric, Earl of Mercia, said nothing else could convince him to lift the heavy taxes he had imposed upon the townspeople.

As soon as she married Edward I, King of England, in 1254, **Eleanor of Castile** insisted on redoing the entire palace with high-priced carpeting from Spain.

To guard against boredom (a common problem in the fifteenth century), **Barbara von Brandenburg,** marchioness of Mantua, amused herself with slaves, a dwarf and a zoo.

Not only did **Beatrice D'Este** make her husband give up all his mistresses, she kept her voluminous wardrobe in closets made-to-order by Leonardo da Vinci.

Among her exploits in the seventeenth century, **Aphra Behn** wandered around Surinam, was captured as a spy, thrown in debtors' prison and wrote several scandalous plays.

In the eighteenth century, **Moscho Tzavella** successfully led the fight against the Turkish Army with a battalion of stick-wielding wimmin from a small Greek village.

Find a Femtor

In 1920, **Elsa Schiaparelli** changed the course of history by inventing the term "shocking pink." She went on to be the first designer to feature padded shoulders, zippers and synthetic fabrics.

The first great woman matador, **Concita Cintron,** killed eight hundred bulls on horseback and four hundred on foot. In 1949, she became an instant pacifist when, after leading her prey through a perfect series of passes, she decided to let the beast go free. She was heavily censured by her male associates and subsequently took up the gentler art of dog breeding.

Helena Wright, who campaigned for birth control, invented disposable diapers after taking her four-month-old baby on the Trans-Siberian railway.

Lesbian swashbucklers **Doña Ana Lezama de Uriza** and **Doña Eustaquia de Sonza** got their kicks from dressing up as caballeros and starting street duels. As luck would have it, their madcap adventures in Peru were bankrolled by an inheritance from Doña Eustaquia's padre.

"Skittles" Walters, a witty and vivacious English courtesan who "entertained" the Prince of Wales, was among the first to take up roller skating in the 1800s.

Amelia Earhart flew across the Atlantic solo carrying only a thermos of hot soup. (Recommended for WASPs only.)

Norma Hanson kicked the teeth out of a great white shark during her hard-hat diving act on Catalina Island and lived to tell the story.

Womyncycles

Ho, womynsisters! Welcome to my nonphallocentric, nonspeciocentric, multicultural processed tree carcass on sacred womynrites.

You're just drooling with anticipation, aren't you?

Because there's only so much honoring and reclaiming you can do all by your lonesome. After a while, you need the loving support of your womynsisters to progress to even higher levels of your heeling program—not to mention higher heels. That's why deep within your innermost self you dream of running about skyclad (naked) with your very own womyncoven. But there's nothing in the yellow pages under goddess rituals and you don't know where to turn, am I right?

Well, you've come to the right place.

The first thing you need to know is that the goddess is the greatest she-babe of all time—in fact, *the* she-babe who *created* Time (and Life and People, but not *Newsweek* or *Play-*

boy). I am speaking of Mother Earth, also known to initiates as Mother Nature.

Now the main thing about her is that she works in cycles. Life and death, night and day, growth and decay. That's why so many really empowered people eat lunch at the Four Seasons every day—*not* to see and be seen, but to honor the Great Mother's sacred cycles.

So, as you might expect, most of your basic goddess rituals are tied into cyclical events. You got your full moons, your new moons, your vernal equinox, your summer solstice, your winter white sales and . . .

You know where this is going, don't you?

You feel the pressure and you want to run. I know, I've been there. But there's no turning back from . . .

Our sacred womyncycles.

Our *femses*.

We are being called upon by our goddess-worshipping sisters to rejoice in our monthly womynflow. To honor the onset of femstruation and femopause.

You heard me. We're being asked to heel our femstrual shame which, besides being a psychotool of the patriarchy, is what causes PFS (formerly PMS).

Are you ready for this?

Maybe I'm totally brainwashed. Maybe *I'm* a psychotool of the patriarchy. Maybe I'm the voice of the goddess backlash, but I just don't get how my monthly misery is the fault of some guy—or even *all* guys of all time. Now, don't get me wrong. I blame guys for making our foremothers feel like filth and banishing them to little huts. I blame guys for making them sit in the river until they stopped being "unclean." I also blame guys for practically everything else that's wrong with my personal life and humyn civilization. But, call me stupid, I just don't see how guys cause PFS.

Because shame is not the major problem here. It's pain and exhaustion and temporary psychosis that really get you down.

A TELLING TALE

Take my friend, Nadine. She was so desperate for relief from her monthly sojourn to Marat-Sade World that she agreed to accompany her friend Latvia Mooncrater to a Wimmin's Wiseblood Ceremony and Hoedown.

Here, in her own words, is Nadine's account of what happened.

"Latvia promised that if I learned to love my period, to welcome it as a sacred expression of my innermost being, then not only would I stop trying to hack my loved ones into little pieces every month, I'd also be able to cut my intake of HoHo's and Ding Dongs *way* down.

"The ceremony was set for Latvia's backyard during a new moon. I was a little nervous because I was PFSing at the time. In fact, earlier that day I had impulsively purchased a dozen pairs of novelty panties in a wide array of sizes. But Latvia assured me that the wimmin would be sympathetic, so I threw my slicker on over my nightie and went anyway.

"First we lit candles and did a little smudging, which was okay, except I was really hungry and there was nothing to eat. Next there were poems about being one with our womyn-cycles and hatching the eggs of the universe into the Red Sea, that sort of thing.

"When my turn came to talk, I couldn't think of a thing to say, so I just sat there for a really long time feeling stupid, then I burst into tears. The wimmin told me to lie down in the center of the circle. They put their hands on me and told me to just let it come—which I did. When I finally stopped blubbering, I asked if anyone had a steak. This is where it gets really confusing, because they thought I was having a spontaneous past-life memory of being burned at the stake, while actually I was fantasizing about a thick juicy filet mignon. But before I could say anything, they started dancing around me in a circle, chanting and 'sweeping' away the pain of my former life.

"Afterward they gave me giant hugs and thanked me for doing such deep healing in their womyncircle. What could I say? I thanked them profusely and drove straight to the nearest Sizzler."

But, alas, Nadine's story doesn't end there.

"Ever since the ritual, Latvia calls every few weeks and says things like 'Aren't you happy you don't have PFS anymore?' I don't have the heart to tell her that it's worse than ever. Now instead of just acting murderous and insane, I also feel like a total failure in the goddess department, not to mention guilt and shame for letting the wimmin down."

This is a classic case of Goddess-Induced Neurosis, which falls under the general clinical heading of Wholeness Deficiency Disorder.

Says Dr. Mildred "Isis" Pierce: "No matter how much you love the goddess, you're still going to turn into a lunatic before the onset of your femstrual flow. The key here is acceptance, accompanied by a Gold Card."

La Poodela Attends a Politically Correct Wimmin's Potluck and Feather Jewelry Sale

It was the darndest evening I ever spent.

My dear old friend Miranda Mildred-Bertha-Bunny (who recently took the first names of her mother and grandmothers as her last) drove up just as I was running out the door.

"Yo, La Poodela!" she yelled from the curb. "Get in. You're coming with me."

I shook my head. "Sorry, Miranda, I've got a manicure in three minutes."

"Femicure," she corrected me, hopping out of her car.

"Honestly, La Pee, you're still in the dark ages, linguistics-wise."

"Where is it I'm *not* going with you?"

She looked upset. "You know, it never occurred to me before, but the expression 'dark ages' is seriously racist. I can't believe I actually said that."

"Is that what you came all the way over here to tell me?" I was now late for my femicure.

"Of course not, silly. I'm taking you to the first meeting of the Wimmin's Postmodern Potluck and Accessories Society. You don't happen to have a large vat of sesame noodles lying around, do you?"

I shook my head. "Fresh out."

"Oh, well, it doesn't matter, it's not like you had a lot of advance notice or anything. They'll understand."

"I don't care if they understand or not, because I'm not going!" I shouted. But I knew I would. Miranda is the most persuasive person I've ever met. She could have a great future as a maniacal cult leader if she wanted one.

Most of the guests were already there when we arrived. Miranda made the introductions: There was Ellenwomon, her partner, Normawomon, and their two-year-old son, Maxwomon; Asteroid and Luna Lee, Shelley Frieda-Florence-Pearl (Miranda's femtor), Moonanne, and—the only true nonconformist in the bunch—Pat. Word spread that Latvia Mooncrater had to take her beloved feline companion to the vet for an emergency hairball operation, hence was running late.

"Doesn't that look incredible!" Miranda said, nudging me toward the food table and a large pile of goo topped with seaweed that looked a little too fresh for comfort.

My heart sank. I was starving. Why is it that most people who claim to love Mother Earth massacre her bounty in their kitchens?

"Before we dig in, there's something Normawomon and

I want to share with you." It was Ellenwomon. From the tone of her voice, I could tell this wasn't going to be any quickie share n' care moment, so I grabbed a seat.

"This morning, when we were down at the beach collecting seaweed for Normawomon's magnificent Lasagne de la Mare, Maxwomon said to us: 'Mommies, why is it called a potluck? What about all the poor people who don't have any food? Do they go to a pot *unlucky?*' Out of the mouths of babes, huh?"

Everyone nodded vigorously at the remarkable child wisdom of Maxwomon—except me: I was mesmerized by the unidentifiable mollusk that had just crawled out from between the layers of lasagne.

"Goddess, I never realized before what a cruel and oppressive ritual the potluck is," whispered Pat, tears streaming down her face.

Moonanne was in touch with her rage. "It plays right into the hands of whitepigmale ego-testicle imperialists," she hissed.

"That's why we decided we've got to come up with an alternative that doesn't oppress differently advantaged individuals," Ellenwomon continued. "Any ideas?"

"How about *dinner?*" I offered brightly, but no one responded. I guess they were searching for something fresh. Something that had never before been uttered by whitepigmale ego-testicle imperialists. Something with a lot more syllables.

"How about collective enjoyment of random foodstuffs that do not contribute to the perpetuation of speciesism?" suggested Shelley Frieda-Florence-Pearl.

"Ho!" Asteroid seconded the motion, but Luna Lee objected.

"That's all well and good if you happen to be a member of the animal kingdom, but it's a little phylumocentric, if you ask me. What about our botanical sisters?"

"You mean, like zucchini?" Moonanne asked.

"Exactly."

Well, this caused quite a pickle. (So to speak.) Nobody wanted to offend the gentle green and yellow beings who are members of an alternative phylum. On the other hand, no one present had yet evolved to the point where she could live on air alone. Finally, it was decided to go with Shelley Frieda-Florence-Pearl's suggestion, but also to honor the botanical individuals who generously lay down their lives to become dead white European male (Caesar) salad.

"Maxwomon is blazing a new trail for his gender." It was the recently arrived Latvia Mooncrater, looking radiant. (Apparently, the hairball operation had been a stunning success.) "He thinks he's a girl."

"What?" I thought maybe I hadn't heard her correctly.

"He thinks he's a *girl*. So far he's never even been in a room with a genetically oppressive individual. Isn't that brilliant?"

I had to sit down. Something cracked, then squished beneath me. It was the renegade mollusk.

"The idea is to breed a new womyn-identified male, a male who will help rebuild the matriarchy," she confided. "In another generation or two, men won't even know they're men!"

She rose and turned toward the food table, then wheeled back around, whispering into my ear, "If you're smart, you'll put all your money into sperm banks. *Now.*"

"Thanks for the tip," I said, and ran for the door.

I could hear Miranda calling after me. "La Pee, where are you going? You haven't tried on any sacred feather jewelry yet or tasted my Apple Betty Friedan!"

But I didn't look back.

Maybe it wasn't too late for my femicure after all.

SAMPLE MENU FOR YOUR VERY OWN POLITICALLY CORRECT POTLUCK

- Oysters Emma Goldman
- A Fish of Non-Color with Green Goddess Sauce
- Momovers
- Stuffed Femicotti
- Gerwomyn Potato Salad
- Scorched Dead Animal Carcass Stroganoff
- Crepes Suzette B. Anthony
- Mommy Seed Cake
- Baby Ruth Ginsburgs
- Humynashevitz Wine

Stand By Your...

Never before in history, recorded or otherwise, have men been so uncool. So unhip. So *superfluous.*

Right now, aliens are more cool than guys. Marie Osmond is more cool than guys. Everybody who isn't a guy is more cool than guys.

You read it here: Men are dead.

The cold truth is, we don't need them anymore: not for breeding, not for support, not for sex and, definitely, not for fun.

"Bu . . . Bu . . . But, La Poodela," I hear you stammer, "can't I be cool *and* stand by my man?"

The answer is no. Not if you want to be hip and make the cover of *Newsweek* or get invited to the really rockin' parties.

But for those weak-willed, retro she-babes (you know who you are) who haven't kicked the guy habit but are dying to make the A-list, here are a few rationalizations you can use to hoodwink your womyn-bonded womynsisters into believing you're really one of them.

Rationalization #1: He's cost effective. It's like having all the advantages of a vibrator *without* having to buy an endless supply of batteries—plus sometimes he pays for dinner.

Rationalization #2: He's got great connections. I'm just using him to get to his sister (mother, aunt, girlfriend, con-gresswomyn).

Rationalization #3: It's just a stage, Part I. Just as soon as the national health insurance bill is passed, he's going to have a sex-change operation.

Rationalization #4: It's just a stage, Part II. I just wanted to see what it was like.

Rationalizations #5, 6, 7: It's not what it looks like. He's gay. He's my brother. He's my grandfather.

Rationalization #8: The mix-up. She's just very butch. (This can only work as long as none of your friends dances cheek to cheek with him, and you never, ever take him anywhere near the beach.)

Rationalization #9: It's a political action. I'm only with him now so I can dump him and torment him later on—the way they've been doing to us ever since Eve was kind enough to offer Adam a nice piece of fruit.

Rationalization #10: There is no rational explanation, only unseen, mysterious forces at work. I can't believe you can actually *see* him. You must be *very* evolved. His name is Dick-ananda and he's my spirit guide.

Part Three

Poodlewoman Meets Iron John

The Politics of Getting Laid

Okay, for whatever pathetic reason, you're still hung up on men.

Maybe you're repressed. Maybe you're a heterosexist. Maybe you should have your head examined.

Then again, maybe not.

Because—suspect as it sounds—you may be a woman who actually *likes* men.

You may even be a woman who likes a *specific* man who likes you back.

Unfortunately, as a layperson who wants to get laid in a world turned upside down by the politics of gender, you're in no position to judge.

Nobody is.

Except me—but only because I'm being guided by Ethel, whose fifty thousand years of dating and marital experience give her something of an edge.

DEAR LA POODELA,

I feel like a real traitor admitting it, but I love my husband, Chuck. He's hot and sexy, plus he does all the laundry *and* brings me roses every Friday. The thing is, every time my friends start bitching about what scum men are, I'm filled with shame. Do you think I'm warped or some kind of addict? Should I join a recovery group for Adult She-Children Who Delude Themselves Into Thinking That Certain Adult He-Children Are Nice? La Poodela, am I nuts? Are all men *ipso facto* pigs or what?

LONI F.
ABILENE, KANSAS

DEAR LONI,

Does Chuck have any friends?

Seriously, doll, your only problem is sociocultural. A few lifetimes from now you'll look back on this period and see how the current rash of man-hating was necessary to balance the weeniecentrism that's been building since Minos. In the meantime, you're one of the lucky ones, so stop with the guilt and enjoy!

Besides, never count your chickens before you know where all the eggs are. For all you know, Chuck may have a couple of wives and thirteen children in Wichita.

DEAR LA POODELA,

I live with a *very* sensitive man. Marcel's been to AA, ACOA, healing circles, men's grief groups and, this very second, he's on his way to a weekend for "Men Who Run With The Women Who Run With The Wolves"—just to please me!

The problem is, I am *not* pleased. To put it bluntly, Marcel is turning into a boneless, gelatinous wuss before my very eyes.

When I told him I wanted him to act more macho (trust me, I couldn't believe my own ears either), he started to weep and asked me if I knew of any "Macho Man" weekends he could sign up for.

Please, La Poodela, help! If it weren't for the fact that he's always off growing somewhere, I don't think I could take it for one more minute.

FED UP
POCAHONTAS, ARKANSAS

DEAR FED UP,

Your only hope is to stimulate the production of testosterone in this man—and believe me, I never thought I'd catch myself saying *that* either! The best

way is through sudden shock. Who knows? It sometimes works for coma victims and, frankly, it sounds as
though Marcel is also missing in action.

There are many creative ways to go about this.

1. Be a woman who runs with the wolves. When Marcel
returns from one of his weekends, let him find you prancing about the house naked with a pack of wolves. This
should provide the shock you're looking for, though not
without a price. In fact, there's a strong possibility that
you'll both be torn limb from limb.

2. Be a woman who runs with Wolf Blitzer. If the above
option strikes you as too risky, substitute the hairy newsman
for the four-legged howling, growling variety.

3. Go on a shopping spree—with Marcel's money. The idea
here is to get your hands on all his assets and cash them in.
Buy a ranch in Wyoming, a palazzo in Venice and, it goes
without saying, a brand new wardrobe off the runways in
Paris. This should put Marcel directly in touch with his lost
manhood. However, unless he's a billionaire, the plan could
backfire—in which case, scale down your expectations and
go hog-wild with his J.C. Penney card.

4. Have sex with his best friend. There's no better way to
activate a guy's male hormones than by having sex with his
best friend. In most cases, it's enough to verbally inform the
man in question of your activities. However, in Marcel's
case, more extreme action is necessary—otherwise this
testosterone-challenged creature is likely to start whimper-
ing and sign up for a jealousy weekend. Thus, to achieve the
desired effect, you must perform the act before his very
eyes and, for best results, on his turf—say, in his office or on
the hood of his car. If he doesn't plug you, smile sweetly
and explain that you're doing it for *him*.

DEAR LA POODELA,

I think I'm losing it. Or maybe I've already lost it. In any case, I need help! Last year I married this terrific guy—Olaf. There's just one problem. He thinks we should spend every single night—plus the *entire* weekend—together. Maybe I'm deranged or something, but this is a concept I just don't get. Like why if I have lots of friends—including guys—am I supposed to want to be with Olaf every second? I mean, it's one thing not to have sex with other people, but *dinner?* Could you please explain your position re: dating and marriage? Hurry!

EMMA B.
PARAMUS, NEW JERSEY

DEAR EMMA,

I'm so glad you brought this up. Let me assure you right off the bat: You are *not* deranged. In fact, as far as I'm concerned, dating during marriage is an absolute must. Nobody, but nobody, wants to have dinner with the same person every single night. If they say they do, they're lying. (If you said you *never* wanted to have dinner with Olaf, I might fear for the longevity of your union.)

Still, whenever the subject of dating and marriage pops up, the question of *whom* to date inevitably follows. What it boils down to is this: Should you date men you're attracted to—thus playing with fire (possibly, great *balls* of fire)—or should you concentrate on nerds and other less-appealing members of the male genus—thereby risking severe boredom?

Your best bet is to hook up with a man you're deeply

attracted to, a man who adores you in return and wants nothing more than to spend every possible second with you—when he's not off having sex with his boyfriend. It's the ideal arrangement: you can flirt to your heart's content, have intimate talks peppered with silences and meaningful gazes. You can even hold hands or plop down on the couch and give each other foot rubs. Best of all, even if you fantasize about sleeping with him (you will), not to worry—he won't return the favor. And, because the relationship will never be consummated, that unspoken "What if?" will always, ever so lightly, perfume the air—adding just the right amount of tension and intrigue.

If, however, there are no dreamy gay prospects waiting in the wings, there are other options—though none with quite the same low-risk, high-satisfaction yield:

Your shrink. The big plus here is that you're expected, even encouraged, to fall in love with him (or her) *and talk about it.* The more the better! This can generate quite a bit of heat, not to mention titillating dreams which—if you really care about your mental health—you must report in painstaking detail. On the down side, not only do you have to fork over your net worth in order to flirt with this person, the relationship—no matter how intimate—is *not* going to lead to dates. If it does, notify the American Psychological Association at once.

Married friends. This can work, but availability—or, rather, lack thereof—is frequently a deterrent. Thus, your time together will be brief and on the fly, and rarely involve just the two of you lingering over pasta. If, however, your married friend is also your close personal colleague, there's always the promise of lunch. But, please note: casual lunches can progress to *long* lunches and, if you're not careful, *really long* lunches served on rolling carts by men in crisp uniforms with tea towels draped over their sleeves.

Single friends. Proceed with caution.

Single strangers, married strangers. Proceed with *extreme* caution.

DEAR LA POODELA,

I'm thinking of moving in with my boyfriend but—and this is a *big* but—I'm not that crazy about housework! The truth is, I'd rather crawl across the desert naked whistling "Zippideedoodah" than spend my life chasing dust bunnies. The thing is, Marvin's a pretty tolerant fellow, but don't all guys secretly expect women to do most of the housework—even if they pretend otherwise?

"BEEBEE"
LAS VEGAS, NEVADA

DEAR "BEEBEE,"

Another of my pet topics!

First of all, let me refer you to a recent front-page story in the *New York Times* which quoted trend-spotters as saying that all across America housework is undergoing a serious decline.

Well, my dear. I've been on the cutting edge of that bandwagon for years! Personally, I've never seen the point of trying to stop the natural process of disintegration. You might just as well try to stop the leaves from falling off the trees.

Viva la entropy!

And I'll let you in on another little secret: dust bunnies are biodegradable; rage and resentment are not.

Which brings us to Marvin.

He'll never admit that he expects you to do more than your share of housework; he just won't do any himself. Nor will he think about it. (And, frankly, any man who obsesses about dust bunnies is suspect in other ways too numerous to go into.) The fact is, no matter how much of a decadent she-slob you are, you will still give more thought to the shambles you call home than Marvin. At least, you'll *see* the mess. He will not. Instead, he'll let the newspapers pile up until they reach the ceiling or you scream at him—whichever comes first. Then he'll apologize and give you that wounded-but-innocent *I-had-no-idea* look and spend the next several hours making like Cinderella before the ball. Afterward, he'll ravish you with kisses and you'll have no choice but to forgive him—whereupon he'll promise to change his wayward ways, then promptly forget his promise.

(This raises the issue of the male memory: Do they have one? The answer is yes, but it's highly selective and does not include the removal of old newspapers or dirty socks.)

In order to reduce domestic hot spots to a minimum, you'll want to rely on service professionals wherever possible. Not only should you refuse to clean the home—and certainly *never* singlehandedly—there are a number of other tactics that will help.

No cooking. For one thing, you can eat more cheaply ordering in than cooking yourself, plus you'll never have to buy soy sauce again. There are other benefits too: Not only will this strategy keep you and Marvin from arguing over who's going to make dinner, you'll form close, first-name friendships with peoples of many nations. In fact, it would not be an exaggeration to consider yourselves informal goodwill ambassadors of the U. S. government—immigration branch.

No shopping. This follows the No-Cooking policy as surely as the night the day.

No laundry. You wouldn't consider for a moment doing your dry cleaning, so why should you do your wet cleaning? There are perfectly nice people who operate tidy and efficient establishments that do it for you. They have mortgages and bills to pay too. They need *your* support.

If you adhere to the principles outlined in this program, I think we can safely predict you won't be crawling across the desert whistling "Zippideedoodah" any time soon.

However, to avoid unnecessarily sticky situations (though not necessarily sticky floors), you should apprise Marvin of your position on housework *before* signing a lease.

DEAR LA POODELA,

Do you think you can still be a feminist if you're in love with a guy who's a descendent of dead white European trash? Please write back ASAP! I can't put Cornelius off much longer.

ANNA O.
VIENNA, VIRGINIA

DEAR MS. O,

Shakespeare Mozart Rilke Shaw
Ot-nay all en-may are ucked-fay, n'est-ce pas?

On the other hand, I'll wager that not one of these boys was a prize when it came to housework.

What Women Really Want (And Why Men Don't Really Want To Know)

Guys have been asking the question, "What do women really want?" since the beginning of time—not because they really want to know, but because they *don't* want to know. That's right. This is their big secret. And up until now they've managed to keep it under wraps.

Actually, the whole thing got started during a "Meet Your Inner Ape" weekend back in the cave when one chest-beating genius by the name of Fredsasquatchhomme came up with the idea that if guys just kept asking the question over and over, women would be hoodwinked into believing that they sincerely wanted to know the answer. On that very same weekend, "Fred" and his grunting hunting pals made

What Women Really Want

a secret pact obliging all men from that day forward to treat women like impossible, irrational, incorrigible creatures and to never, ever let on that, actually, they have a pretty good idea of what women really want.

There are many reasons for this. For one thing, guys get a lot of mileage out of playing dumb. How many times have you given men what *they* want—which has *never* been a matter for speculation, not even for a second—just for being sensitive enough to ask the question?

Of course, what most women since Eve have failed to notice is that just because they *ask* doesn't mean that any guy living or dead has ever paid attention to the answer.

Because if they did, they'd never have anything to say to each other since, next to activities that involve balls of many shapes and sizes, guys love to talk about how they're completely baffled by women. Where would they be without such witty sentiments as this one from Lawrence Durrell:

"There are only three things to be done with a woman. You can love her, suffer for her or turn her into literature." Or the gangster version, from *Prizzi's Honor,* in which Jack Nicholson, considering his future with Kathleen Turner, says, "I don't know whether to ice her or marry her."

But even more than the fear of having their best lines taken away, the main reason guys will never admit to having even the teensiest clue about what women really want is because if they did, they'd have to *do something about it.*

In this case, knowledge would definitely *not* be power and the weeniecentric universe men know and love would be more threatened than ever.

But as long as guys plead ignorance, they figure we'll continue to believe that they're just a bunch of well-meaning but bumbling doofuses who don't know any better.

Sorry, boys. The jig is up.

TWELVE STEPS TO HAPPINESS WITH A WOMAN

Here, *one more time,* is the answer to the age-old question, *so listen up . . .*

Women *really* want men to:

1. Listen. That's right. When women speak—especially when we use a language in which the man to whom we're speaking is fluent—we expect him to pay attention and

2. Hear what we say. This can be acknowledged in a variety of ways, tailored to meet the individual male's personal style of communication. A simple yes, uh-huh, nod of the head or even a grunt will do. Staring blankly into space, however, will not get you far.

3. Respond. This is the tough part and depends on successfully completing Steps One and Two. The key here is to respond to what was just said, not what was said three weeks ago. For example, if a woman says "I want pizza for dinner," that means she wants pizza for dinner—even though the last twelve times you suggested pizza, she made a face and ate tuna salad instead.

4. Mean what you say. Who knows, maybe we're just too damn literal for our own good but—preposterous as it seems—women expect men to mean what they say. "I'll call you tomorrow" does *not* mean "Don't ever expect to hear from me again" or "Maybe I'll call you a week from Thursday if it's raining and I have nothing better to do."

5. Say what you mean—*not* what you think she wants to hear, *not* what you think will make her happy, *not* what will keep her from screaming at you and calling you a loathsome, insensitive asshole. Do I make myself clear?

6. Tell the truth. Always remember that when you *don't* tell the truth, she'll find out anyway. This is one of the few absolutes in the universe you can really count on. And, when she does find out, not only will she be pissed at you for whatever it was you did (or didn't do), she'll be furious that you lied to her about it.

7. Don't leave out anything she would consider really important, even if it means nothing to you. Don't kid yourself, telling a woman that you stopped by the local pub on your way home, but neglecting to mention that you spent the entire time with a teen model named Daphne in the back of her Jeep Cherokee is the same as telling a lie.

8. Remember stuff. Don't expect her to believe that the same guy who remembers how many bases Jackie Robinson stole during the 1955 World Series is incapable of remembering which night you're having dinner with her mother or where your dirty socks go.

9. Anticipate. This technique is also called "thinking ahead." Here's how it works. Say you notice that the milk carton is empty. Would you (1) buy some more on your way home from work? (2) pray that the cow fairy will visit your apartment? (3) expect your loved one to take care of it? (4) decide to give up cereal and eat jelly donuts for the rest of your life?

10. Take initiative. Remember when you and your beloved first started seeing each other? You asked her out. You picked the restaurant. You made reservations. Once you even bought tickets to a show. How long has it been since you've done any of these things? Why not? How about tonight?

11. Go with the flow. Sometimes she cries, sometimes she laughs, sometimes her hormones turn her into a killer tomato. And you never know what's coming, do you? Well, stop trying to figure it out, because you never will. A woman takes after her mother—Nature, that is. Don't expect her to behave the way she did last week. That was then. She lives in the now. Try to keep up.

12. Surrender to Your Higher Power. Her. Always remember, you're one lucky guy to be allowed to get this close to the sacred primal forces of the universe. Don't blow it.

AND DON'T FORGET . . .

Now that we've covered the first twelve steps to happiness with a woman, it's time to get down to specifics.

- Familiarize yourself with the layout of your home. If you don't know where the kitchen is, stop and ask for directions.
- While we're on the subject, when you're lost *outside* the home, stop and ask for directions then too.

- Try not to confuse the woman in your life with your mother, your ex-girlfriend or Charles Barkley.
- Provide a high level of services. This includes, but is not limited to, dealing with all dead things from steak and garbage to vermin.
- Living vermin are your department too.
- Buy gifts that suggest that you have at least some rudimentary knowledge of the recipient's identity.
- When out to dinner and waiting for your table, pretend you're a stranger and try to pick her up while you're sitting at the bar. (This move is guaranteed to score you big points.)
- Though from time to time (and especially first thing in the morning) the woman in your life will engage in a spiritual practice known as "Meeting the Inner Hag," pretend not to notice.
- If you value your life, never, ever make the following remark to a woman—not even your best friend: "I'm not in that much of a hurry. I guess I'm lucky I don't have a biological clock to worry about."
- Now that you've mastered the art of putting the toilet seat down, it's time to start cleaning those little facial hairs out of the sink.
- Get some friends. You need somebody to pour your heart out to besides your wife or girlfriend. Conversations centered around ball sports don't count. And, in case you were wondering, a close friend is somebody you talk to more than twice a year.
- Learn how to tell time. Women don't enjoy hanging out on street corners.
- Never wear orange or plaid and—under no circumstances—in the same outfit.

- Fondle the woman in your life once for every thousand times you play with your private parts. That should be just about right.

- Just so you know, it's humanly possible to cuddle *without* penetration.

- A good memory is an important sexual attribute. Remember how she told you she likes it? Good.

- Just in case you were out to lunch when she mentioned it, women favor light, flicking motions during oral sex. If you catch yourself making like a vacuum cleaner, don't kid yourself—it's strictly projection.

- Women like aural sex too: Tell her you love her. Talk dirty to her. Talk to her.

- Never forget that the woman you are with is the most incredible sex goddess who ever lived. Treat her accordingly.

La Poodela's Little Guide To The Testosterone Enhanced

Confusing isn't it? And scary! All that testosterone out there, running amok! It's hard to know which guys are going to turn into werewolves after the first date—and, let's face it, *nobody* wants to be a woman who runs with the werewolves, am I right?

Well, you've come to the right place for guidance.

Because before you can find Mr. Right, you've got to find the Mr. Right Archetype.

Mr. Wingspan (aka Iron John). After years of calling himself a feminist, he now feels justified in hating women again—and, boy, is it fun! The fact is, he hates everybody who ever stifled the free expression of his Inner Hairy Beast. The list of the Ten Most Despised includes Mom, who turned him into a wuss; Dad, who was never around to teach him to

Poodlewoman Meets Iron John

hunt or smelt on account of that rotten old Industrial Revolution; his older sister, who made him play Tinkerbell to her
Peter Pan; and all the needy, conniving she-beasts who ever
wanted to tame him and call him "hon." Though this nou-
veau, PC Marlboro Man may at times seem self-assured and
on top of things, watch out. His "wound" is still actively oozing and—no matter what—he'll never let you come
between him and his sacred tom-tom.

Mr. Womynspirit is the New Age he-feminist ("We're all a
perfect manifestation of the Oneness") *before* Iron John
weekend. Oh, what a sensitive being! Oh, what a tender
soul! Even though personally he doesn't have to deal with
wildcat hormones, he'll weep over *your* PMS—which, in that
uncanny, psychic way of his, he *knows* is a direct result of
that lifetime in the fourteenth century when your name was

Gundrun and you died in childbirth. (He oughta weep—he was Yggdrasil, the wall-eyed midwife who botched the delivery!) If you can tolerate the depth of his caring and sharing, Mr. Womynspirit makes an ideal best friend. But no matter how close you get—beware. Sooner or later, he's going to sign up for an Iron John Intensive. He too will spend time in the forest grieving the Industrial Revolution that turned strong and powerful men into panty-hose salesmen. He too will learn to hate you anew.

Mr. Space Case might actually benefit from a male-bonding weekend but, alas, he'll never be able to find the application, let alone postage and a mailbox. The good news is that if he ever actually went, he wouldn't come back and hate you. On the down side, he might not come back at all. The biggest risk with this guy is not losing him to his tribal brothers or another woman, it's losing him—period. A tracking device is recommended to keep him within range, especially in public places, such as malls and bustling foreign capitals. On the up side, when he's not out to lunch, Mr. Space Case can be fun, sweet and even attentive, though he does have a habit of drifting off in mid-sentence or mid-task, such as mowing the lawn. (Luckily, when it comes to sex, once he gets going, he has no trouble crossing the finish line.) The big mystery here is how the same guy who couldn't find five items on a grocery list if his life depended on it can run the show at work.

Mr. (Center of the) Universe. Just like Louis XIV, he's the Son King—and, just in case you forget, his sainted mother, the Lint Queen, will always be within spitting distance to remind you. Still, if there are any gaps in your knowledge, not to worry, Mr. Universe will be happy to fill you in, because *he knows everything!* And being the generous guy he is, he loves to share. (Okay, so maybe there are a *few* little things he doesn't like to share, like the items listed on the prenuptial agreement he hands out to prospective dates but, hey, that doesn't mean he's not an altruist in his own way!) The good news and the bad news: You'll never lose him at the mall.

Mr. Marlboro Light. Your ideal companion in practically any natural disaster: earthquakes, tornadoes, floods and—especially—stampedes! He's Bogart, he's Mitchum, he's Indiana Jones. He's Iron John *without* the hugging. Lucky for him, the Industrial Revolution never cramped *his* manhood. And the good news is, he doesn't hate you! In fact, he loves you—as long as you look and act like a woman (and break just like a little girl!). But even though he could benefit from a "Bonsai Appreciation" or "Art of French Pastry" weekend, the New Age has not left him untouched. Nosiree, Clint! He expresses his newfound sensitivity every single day when he orders his Bud Lite and—if he's really trying to impress a gal—a turkeyburger!

Mr. Snugli. He's perfect in every way. The perfect husband. The perfect father. (You'd snap him up for either in a New York minute!) In fact, he's the only man you've ever met who strikes the perfect balance between sensitivity and testosterone. Trouble is, he's all booked up for this lifetime. The best you can hope for is that he's your shrink—in which case—who knows?—several years of intensive therapy and you might just get your foot in the door for the next lifetime.

Mr. Wrong Again. He has everything: dark velvety eyes, a smoky voice, an accent. One night he calls you on the spur of the moment and says, "Meet me in Budapest." You leave at once. You travel all night and half the next day. When at last you arrive, exhausted, exhilarated, a bottle of Dom Perignon is waiting. A basket of wild irises is waiting. He's waiting. The world drops quietly out of sight. It's just the two of you now.

There is no Time. Only Love. Until the next morning when the phone rings. On the way to the airport your driver, a kindly, bespectacled man called Pavel, offers you a tissue. Gratefully, you accept. Oh, well, you tell yourself, as you watch the city disappear, you'll always have Budapest. And he'll always have his wife.

Mr. Right At Last. This guy's the compleat catch: adorable, fit, stylish, smart, generous, funny—the original Irony John. And he's single! Not only that, he cooks, he dances, he loathes football, he cries at all the right places in movies, he even *works* for a living! And he'll happily spend hours with you discussing the Royals—Lady Clairol, Dame Edna, Boy George. But, wait, there's more! He loves the same books, the same music, but best of all, he loves *you!* Yes, *you!*—without ambivalence. He's committed to you for life. And, believe it or not, his *mother* adores you too. She's already got her dress for your wedding all picked out. Things couldn't be more perfect. There's just one small hitch.

So who needs sex, anyway?

The Date

A Tragicomedy in One Act

Dating just isn't what it used to be. Now not only do you have to deal with all those wacky guy archetypes, you've got your *inner* lineup to contend with too.

Setting:	Your mind and your apartment, simultaneously.
Time:	The present, around midnight.
Dramatis Personae:	You
	Your Inner Selves
	Marvin, an unmarried endodontist
Marvin:	(*At your front door*) Can I come in?
You:	Uh . . .

Inner Tina Turner:	Puhleez, girl . . .
Inner Mother:	Not so fast! She may never get another date!
Inner Gloria Steinem:	So what? You think she needs a *man* for self-esteem?
Inner Sugar Daddy:	Ask him how much he takes home *after* malpractice insurance.
Marvin:	(*Several minutes later*) Well?
New Inner Mother:	Whatever you say is fine. You're a beautiful empowered daughter of Mother Earth.
You:	Okay. But just for a few minutes.
Marvin:	(*Entering*) You know, you're a very thoughtful person. Whenever I ask you a question, you really take your time to mull it over. I respect that. (*Sitting on the couch and patting the seat cushion next to him*) Come here.
Inner Tina:	No way, Jose . . .
Inner Mother:	Wait a minute, as unbelievable as it seems, he *likes* her. An actual living, breathing man likes *my* daughter. I think I'm going to have a heart attack.
Marvin:	(*Winking*) Come on, I don't bite . . .
Inner Child:	Ick! Yuck! I want my blanky!
Inner Bimbo:	(*To Inner Child*) What is it with your blanky? Why can't we just close our eyes and pretend he's Mel or Alec!
You:	I'll be right back. I have to go to the bathroom. (*Rushing out of the room*)

Inner Groucho: Hey, did you hear the one about the dyslexic-agnostic insomniac?

Inner Mother: Don't pay any attention to him. Hurry up and get back out there, you dope! It could be love!

Inner Tina: (*Singing*) "What's love got to do, got to do with it?"

Inner Groucho: He stayed up all night worrying that there was no dog.

You: (*Entering*) Ha ha.

Marvin: What's so funny?

Inner Existentialist: Go ahead and laugh. Even a good joke can't stop Death. Or Marvin.

You: You know, Marvin, even a good joke can't stop death.

Marvin: God, you're deep. (*Moving closer*) That's why I can relate to you. I'm deep too. (*Staring into her eyes*) Why do you think I went into root canal? (*He tries to kiss her*)

Inner Child: Help! I'm gonna throw up!

Inner Tina: Get his sorry ass outta here!

Inner Gloria: NOW!

Marvin: What's the matter?

You: Goodnight, Marvin. (*Pushing him away*)

Marvin: But why? We have so much in common.

Inner Mother: Don't let him get away! What's wrong with you?

Inner Nazi:	I'll tell you what's wrong with her. She's the most negative person who ever walked the earth plane.
Inner Existentialist:	Negative! I think it's a miracle she doesn't blow her brains out.
New Inner Mother:	Repeat after me: "I am a magnificent and whole womyngoddess."
You:	(*Screaming*) Stop it! All of you! I can't take it anymore!
Marvin:	Now what? What did I do? (*He's being shoved out the door*) Wait . . . !
You:	*Goodnight,* Marvin . . .
Inner Groucho:	Hey, did you hear the one about the opera singer who got a canary stuck in her epiglottis?
Marvin:	You're making a terrible mistake. I think we could really have something. Aren't you sick of being alone?
You:	(*Slamming the door*) I only wish!
Inner Groucho:	(*Chomping on his cigar*) That's funny. I never heard that one either. (*He winks*)

BLACKOUT

Indigenous Chic
A Guided Experience for Couples

Have you noticed how everybody seems to have discovered the Native Indigenous Peoples of North America* lately? It's like the Second Coming of Columbus, only this time we're trying to make up for all the rotten things we did to them by *becoming* them!

Now, instead of killing them and stealing their land or making fun of them on TV, we're running all over the place smudging each other's auras, passing the talking stick and shouting ho!

This is all fine, I suppose—goddess knows, Indigenous Peoples have plenty to teach us. But it must be a tad confus-

---

*Native Indigenous Peoples is now the preferred term, since Native American contains a reference to that dead white European scoundrel-explorer, Amerigo Vespucci.

ing for them to watch their culture—previously despised and ridiculed—turn suddenly chic.

It's also more than a tad ironic that in order to heal our wounded inner selves, we're turning to the traditions, symbols and ancestors of cultures we know little about, while rejecting our own ancestors and symbols.

Then again, it's not all that hard to understand why wholeness seekers might prefer to embrace Pocahontas and Crazy Horse over General Custer and Attila the Hun.

But not everyone is equipped to trade their lox and bagels for buffalo and beans. Not everyone is prepared to sacrifice their air-conditioned houses and Jeeps in order to live closer to Great Spirit.

Luckily, there *is* an alternative.

If you want to get in on the action but aren't ready to leave your world behind, perhaps you should consider adopting the ways of one of the more modern tribes—the *Lakota Jioux*.

Unlike the Navajos, Hopis and Lakota *Sioux*, who still practice the ancient traditions the old-fashioned way, the Jioux have—for your pleasure and personal growth—adapted those same traditions for the twenty-first century.

Yesiree, Running Poodle! Now, you can have your maize—but *you don't have to eat it!*

Here, then, is the blueprint for your Nouvelle Native Experience, Couples Version, handed down by Jioux elders and revealed for the very first time in these pages.

Step One: Choosing Your Power Animal

What animal really speaks to you? Is it living or stuffed? Free to roam or fricassee? If you don't have a clue, go to the zoo. Talk to the animals. See who talks back. (Remember: Communication with members of the animal kingdom is greatly enhanced by peanuts and popcorn.)

Step Two: The Sweat Lodge

A sweat lodge—or *shvitz*—is a great way to rid your body-mind of pollution and, if you're involved in a toxic relationship, just think of the poisons the two of you can release together! Recommended sites for this sacred ritual: Canyon Ranch, The Golden Door, your local YM & YWHA.

Step Three: Sundance

Though this ceremony has recently fallen into disrepute due to the growing ozone hole in Father Sky, serious seekers cannot afford to miss it. Here's how it works: find a sandy beach. Set out two plastic lounge chairs—or better yet, get a bronze beach stud named Rocco to set them out for you. Take turns slathering sacred oil all over each other. (Warning: Unless your skin is as dark as Rocco's, future passion may be severely curtailed if sacred oil with SPF under 15 is used.) Now take your places on the lounge chairs and honor the four directions by spending equal time on your stomach, back, right side, left side. (Note: Though the Sundance may be performed anywhere the sun shines, to receive full benefits head for one of the tribe's power points: South Beach, East Hampton, the Dead Sea.)

Step Four: Shamanic Journey

Time now to leave the "real" world for the hidden universe where myth is truth and spirits guide you. The first myth to be dispelled is that the Jioux don't drink. As far as spirits are concerned, you can't go wrong with single malt scotch.

Step Five: Full Moon Ceremony

Now that you're purified, it's time for you and your beloved to join other members of the Jioux for a Full Moon Ceremony. This ritual, sometimes called a Charity Benefit, allows the tribe to express its compassion for Mother Earth and her peoples while deepening contact with spirit and beluga.

And—because no ritual would be complete without it—dancing to the primitive beat of Woody Herman and his Thundering Herd.

Step Six: The Medicine Wheel

What a day! Tears and laughter, deep healing rituals. As you meditate on your journey, make a circle of your medicines and sit in the center. What do you need now to help you along your path? Do you have heartburn? A migraine? Gas? Be your own shaman and choose.

Step Seven: Vision Quest

All the rigorous practices you've performed up to this point have been but preparation for the most sacred ritual of all: the Vision Quest. And because we're born alone and die

The Medicine Wheel

alone, so must we undertake the Vision Quest alone (or, possibly, with ten or twelve of our closest friends). The good news is that, unlike the Sioux who do their Questing in the wilderness, the Jioux (who are known to be an adventurous people) do it in department stores, at trading posts, in duty-free shops, in teeming markets, on arduous treks through the Orient and—especially—in Italy and Spain. Get ready, get set, ho!

Step Eight: Honoring the Ancestors

Even though it may be impossible to stand, let alone walk, after your strenuous Vision Quest, you must never forget your heritage. The time has come for you and your beloved to honor the ancestors by showing them—and sometimes trying on and prancing about in—the fruits of your Quest. Warning: In order to receive the blessings of the ancestors, you must assure them that every single fetish and pelt you collected on your journey was an absolute "steal." One last piece of advice: Unless they're stuffed or broiled, leave your power animals at home. The ancestors are deathly allergic to dander.

Men Are From Lemuria, Women Are From Atlantis

It's really something, isn't it, how everybody from Bill Clinton to Roseanne Arnold is going public with their childhood wounds.

Too bad folks living back in the olden days didn't know what we know. Imagine what life would have been like for Dionysus and his pals if they'd spent their nights going to AA and Sex Addicts meetings instead of frolicking down at the old bacchanal. In fact, the history of the western world might have been one long, uninterrupted lovefest if only Judas Iscariot had had a safe place to discharge his rage.

And what about relationships? How many dysfunctional couples could have saved themselves and their children a whole lot of grief work if they'd had the loving support they needed to own their pain? It's inspiring to imagine what miracles might have occurred if they'd been lucky enough to live in the late twentieth century!

Adam and Eve. These two were obvious candidates for Sex and Love Addicts Anonymous, as well as nutritional and sartorial counseling. And if they could have found a decent therapist to help them deal with the trauma of being kicked out of the Garden, we'd all have to do a lot less grief work today. Only one question remains: If addictive behavior is a response to growing up in a dysfunctional family, what does that say about their Father?

Jason and Medea. No family in history makes a more compelling case for child-abuse prevention than the Argonauts. If Jason and Medea had gotten in touch with how they projected their childhood wounds on to each other, maybe he wouldn't have dumped her for that submissive little tart. And even if he had, Medea might have found a more productive way to express her rage than by butchering her children, not to mention the poor tart.

Adam and Eve in Couple's Therapy

Nick and Nora Charles. This besotted duo, who loved nothing more than tripping the light fantastic with smart-mouthed criminals, would become permanent residents of the Betty Ford Center. The mutt, Asta, would be adopted by pious teetotalers from New Hampshire who would put an immediate stop to its antics on the nightclub circuit.

Antony and Cleopatra. What a desperate pair of romance addicts these two were! The world was truly their oyster—he ran Asia, she was in charge of Egypt!—and what did they do? They traded everything for love—a progressive and, in their case, *fatal* disease. Instead of owning their narcissism and destructive behavior, they lolled about the Mediterranean, *shtupping* and feeding each other grapes. The tragedy is, we'll never know if a last-minute jingle to the Suicide Hot Line could have saved their hides.

Romeo and Juliet. First of all, if est training had been available, the good Signors Capulet and Montague would have taken full responsibility for their parts in the dispute and resolved it long before anybody drank poison. Romeo and Juliet would have been free to date—after thorough birth-control counseling—and would have outgrown each other by age sixteen, at which time they'd have both realized they were gay. Romeo would have set off at once for Florence with the divine Mercutio, and Juliet would have split for Rome with Nurse.

Vladimir and Estragon. Have you ever encountered such clinically depressed, codependent enablers as these two clowns? Enough already with the waiting, the kvetching, the waiting, they should go to a clinic, get a prescription for Prozac and get on with it!

Snow White and the Seven Dwarfs. The first really modern family. Unfortunately, they didn't know it. If only the tale had been written today, so much would be different. For starters, the title would be *A Womyn of Non-color and the Seven Vertically Challenged Individuals.* And the individuals themselves would be transformed from victims to survivors. We'd have Difficult to Serve (Grumpy), Differently Awake (Sleepy), Cerebrally Challenged (Dopey), Nasally Different (Sneezy) and Uniquely Friendly (Bashful). As for those two oppressors, Happy and Doc, they'd be renamed Temporarily Emotionally Satisfied and Person. The story itself would become an inspiring tale of recovery: As soon as the vertically challenged individuals heard the Womyn of Non-color's account of her abuse at the hands of her Morally Different Stepmother, they'd see to it that she entered treatment at once. During the long process of getting in touch with her rage and eventually her forgiveness, the Womyn of Non-color would finally heal her Cinderella Complex—the fantasy that someday her prince would come. And having achieved psychological wholeness she would remain in the little hut, devoted to the Vertically Challenged Individuals for as long as she was metabolically abled.

Lucy and Ricky Ricardo. With affirmative action sweeping the nation, Ricky would eventually have to give in to Lucy's demand to be a nightclub performer. Her days of dressing up like a table in order to sneak into the Tropicana would be over; her rise to stardom, meteoric. This would create a serious midlife crisis for the Cuban bandleader, who would be forced to own the pain of being less talented and successful than his wife. He'd have no choice but to take a leave from the club to do some heavy grief work. And, who knows? His gift with the bongos might win him a leadership position in the men's movement.

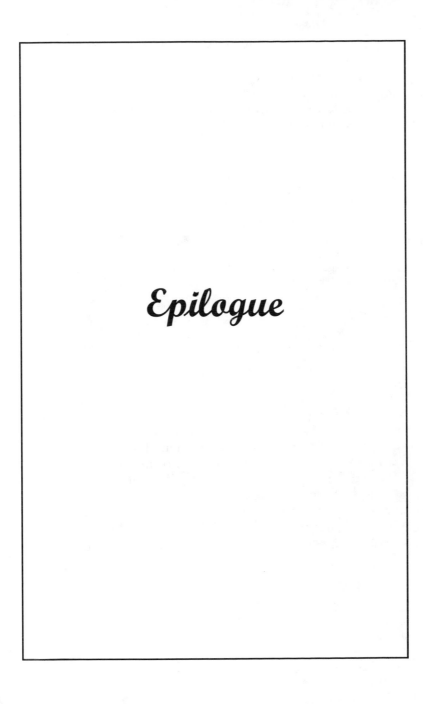

Epilogue

The Last Self-Help Fairy Tale

Once upon a time, there were three Indian princesses: Cries Her Eyes Out, Eats Like A Horse, and Worries Herself Sick. (Actually there was a fourth princess, Laughs Herself Silly, but she was too busy rollicking in the grass and peeing in her pants to pay any attention to her unhappy sisters.)

For they were just like their names: sad, fat and fearful.

And no matter how hard they tried to be happy and whole, nothing worked.

No potions or elixirs, no diets or exercise programs, no

new moon or old constellation rituals—not even bio-psychoangelic therapy or support groups for Indian Princesses Who Wished They Were Dead.

There was nowhere to turn.

No workshop left untried.

No hope that someday things might be different.

So they packed their tiny valises, bade good-bye to the village of their birth and disappeared into the forest.

While they were waiting to die—which took much longer than anyone expected—Cries Her Eyes Out wept mammoth lakes, Eats Like A Horse stockpiled nuts and berries, and Worries Herself Sick built a lookout tower in the trees to keep an eye out for the pack of Big Bad Wolves who were said to roam the forest.

Finally, one starless, moonless night when the princesses were nearing the end and too weak to weep or eat or worry, the wolves came. They circled the dying maidens.

"Go ahead," whispered Cries Her Eyes Out.

"Get it over with," begged Eats Like A Horse.

"Now," said Worries Herself Sick, her voice faint with approaching death.

And so the sisters clasped each other's frail little hands and said farewell.

With that, the wolves reared up on their hind legs and their howls shook the trees and the stars, and all the little creatures who dwelled in the forest fled for cover as the hungry beasts prepared to pounce.

But then the strangest thing happened. Instead of binging on Indian Princess, the wolves wheeled about sharply and leapt off into the night.

The princesses were stunned. Cries Her Eyes Out began to laugh. Eats Like A Horse grabbed a fistful of leaves, but couldn't stop smiling long enough to swallow. Worries Herself Sick whistled at the moon.

And so it was for the very first time since they were born, the sisters were glad to be alive.

At first light they hooked elbows and crawled back to the village on their bellies. Ironically, when Laughs Herself Silly saw them coming, she was so overcome by hysteria and mirth that she rolled off a mesa and—much to everyone's horror—split her sides laughing.

But the story doesn't end here.

The princesses did not marry handsome princes and spend the rest of their lives happily redecorating their tipis. The truth is, they didn't live happily ever after at all.

They were the same miserable lot they'd always been.

Cries Her Eyes Out continued to wail and flail. Only now instead of wasting her tears, she traveled the seven continents turning arid deserts into lush farmland.

And even though Worries Herself Sick still suffered from eczema, migraines and a spastic colon, she put her talents to work for a large security concern, where she eventually became chairprincess and CEO.

As for Eats Like A Horse, she opened a successful taqueria on the outskirts of Tucumcari, New Mexico, and slaved over a hot stove perfecting the world's biggest burrito for as long as she could squeeze through the door.